D0769360

The Making of the Reparation and Economic Sections of the Treaty

The Making of the Reparation and Economic Sections of the Treaty

by

BERNARD M. BARUCH

HOWARD FERTIG

New York · 1970

HOWARD FERTIG, INC. EDITION 1970
Published by arrangement with Harper & Row, Inc.

Library of Congress Catalog Card Number: 68-9615

PRINTED IN THE UNITED STATES OF AMERICA
BY NOBLE OFFSET PRINTERS, INC.

CONTENTS

To
My American Associates
And to My Colleagues in the
Allied and Associated Governments
at the Peace Conference
In Remembrance
of days
crowded with vital endeavor
in which they labored with
a common purpose
to compose
the affairs of a troubled world
I dedicate this volume

INTRODUCTION.

The Human Equation in the Making of the Peace Treaty.

Much misconception exists and many misstatements of fact have been made regarding the reparation and economic sections of the Treaty of Peace—clauses vital to the interest of the American people and even more vital to world stability. As I was intimately concerned with the creation of these sections, my purpose herein is to set forth the problems which the writers of the sections had to meet and why they met them as they did rather than in the various ways suggested by present-day critics.

Before, however, the subject matter of the clauses in question is presented to the reader, it is essential that he should have a mental picture of the conditions under which they were brought into being.

The mightiest conflict of mankind had just come to an end. The cannon's sound had but lately died away; the shock of battle was still upon the world; the aroused primitive passions of nations and of men had only in a small measure subsided; the world's wounds still bled.

Within a few hours' travel from the Peace Conference were the battlefields upon which lay 900,000 dead Englishmen and colonials; 1,300,000 dead Frenchmen; and the bodies of hundreds of thousands of other Allies. On these fields had been sustained the grievous wounds of many millions of living men.

From wantonly devastated France had not departed the fear and inherent hatred of the enemy who but a few months before had pierced almost to her heart—the traditional enemy who had brought upon her the bitter days of 1870. With the World War already history, the shadow of the Prussian still hung over the Republic. France was fixed in her determination to erect an impregnable wall, economic or geographical, or both, against future German invasion. This, in greater or lesser measure, was the attitude of the other Allies.

Outraged Belgium was no less outraged, no less fearful. England and her colonies, that without stint had given of their best in men and the bedrock resources of an empire, trembled from their four years' travail. Italy, shaken and depleted by her long-sustained efforts, had barely escaped the German heel. Of the smaller Allies, Serbia, Rumania, and Poland had been the victims of merciless German aggression. All of the Allies and Associated Governments were bending under the cumulative burdens that had been the price of victory.

In France alone there was not a home that had not been seared by the baleful touch of modern war—a terrible, irrevocable fact in substance true of the other Allied countries. Not only in millions of homes had the breadwinner or the son been annihilated, but many homes after the war held pitiful shattered fragments of once sturdy men, now become the apotheosis of living death.

France came out of the conflict with 1,700,000 wounded men. Their presence kept the memory of the war a fiercely burning flame, to which the powerful emotion of vengeance but added fuel. Facts such as these do not make for cool reasoning; they make for irresistible and elemental human reactions. They had to be reckoned with at Paris. They have to be reckoned with now.

Without exception, the late antagonists of Germany were facing almost unbelievable financial conditions, seemingly impossible of solution without crushing their whole economic and industrial existence. In order to meet, to grapple with, and to remedy these conditions, they would have to resort to taxation methods that appeared humanly out of the question to endure, to drastic readjustments of the entire fabric of their national life.

Relief from this burdensome taxation had been promised from time to time by the leaders in the various countries. These promises in many instances were based upon false and exaggerated ideas of Germany's capacity to pay.

Further, one must realize the impaired and in many instances destroyed economic life of the Allied Powers—a depletion and destruction which made the ensuing burdens seem impossible. Germany had swept over Belgium and northern France. She had ruined mines; she had destroyed factories or removed machinery; she had devastated homes and farms; and she had either appropriated to her own purpose or driven away domestic animals.

Wherever, on land or on sea or in the air, the German power had been exercised, it had left an aftermath of misery or bitterness or hate.

Public opinion in the various Allied and Associated countries had been aroused to a white heat of fear, hatred, and distrust. Facing these facts, one can easily realize the impossibility of arriving at a treaty free from passion and a sense of wrong.

The Allied leaders had agreed to a peace upon the basis of President Wilson's address of January 8, 1918 (containing the Fourteen Points) and the principles of settlement enunciated in his subsequent addresses. These principles had been formulated not in the interest of Germany, but to promote the real interest of the Allies themselves and to advance the cause of world peace and future security. Nevertheless, at an election held after the armistice and agreement as to the basic terms of peace, the English people, by an overwhelming majority, returned to power their Prime Minister on the basis of an increase in the severity of these terms of the peace, especially those of reparation.

The French position, as evidenced by the expressions of the press of all political parties and by the speeches of the Deputies, showed an equally exacting attitude as to reparations. The apparently unanimous sentiment of the French people was perhaps typified in the placards which, during the days of the Peace Conference, covered the walls of Paris and of other cities, proclaiming, *Que L'Allemagne paye d'abord* (Let Germany pay first). The French Government, in fact, found it impossible during the months following the armistice to secure the adoption of any immediate taxation measures by the Chamber of Deputies. This body very justly insisted that the burdens of the war should in the first instance be assumed by Germany.

No one can understand the peace treaty who does not know and cannot measure the human conditions under which it was brought forth. It is singular but true that peace seemed very beautiful during the war, but almost hateful when the war ended. From a superficial survey of the conditions that prevailed at the Peace Conference, one would have been quite justified in assuming that many of the participants preferred war with all its horrors to any peace short of that which they demanded. Their demands had their genesis in deep-rooted and almost ineradicable hatreds and in the insistent desire for self-protection against future danger.

Not a few among the Allies were so intent upon momentary gains as to imperil the entire structure of world-peace, which after all was the real purpose of the Conference. Though the peace delegates individually were able and high-minded, they were bound to the wheel of their national aspirations. Therefore they were unable or unwilling to yield on questions that concerned their own national advantages or safeguards against future German aggressions.

If the ideal peace, which some demand, had been actually undertaken, with all that it seemingly involved of sacrifice and unselfishness, the result would have been the overthrow of at least three of the major governments. It would have been followed further by the substitution of other representatives who would have come into power under a popular mandate requiring them to be even more exacting in their terms.

I call attention to the record on this point, which shows that approximately three hundred members of the House of Commons addressed a telegram to the British Prime Minister demanding fulfillment of the terms promised in the khaki campaign pledges and requiring him to proclaim his intentions. So compelling was the despatch that he was under the necessity of returning to London to reassure the House of his intention to insist upon exacting fullest compliance with the demands that had been formulated in the heat of war passion and during the excitement of a general election.

For further example, Premier Hughes of the Australian Commonwealth insisted that every Australian who had placed a mortgage on his house to buy a war bond was as definitely entitled to reparation as was every Frenchman whose house had been burned by the Germans.

These two examples are concrete indications of the conditions with which the writers of the reparation clauses had to contend. A different story might have been told and a different treaty written if some of the critics had had the courage, clarity, and force to impress their present-day views upon their own representatives at Paris. But the Americans and others had the charity to remember that the horrors of war were still heavy upon the world. Try as men might, and I submit that they did try, the spirit of vengeance or of selfish advantage could not be entirely eradicated from the minds of the framers of the treaty. On them the pressure of public opinion in their respective countries was being constantly exerted.

In the reparation clauses, the Conference was not writing a mere contract of dollars and cents; it was dealing with blood-raw passions still pulsing through the people's veins. It was impossible, I repeat, to ignore the human factors, but provision was made whereby they could be reduced or eliminated later and whereby the Reparation Commission in the processes of enforcement might become a flexible instrument of wisdom and justice.

There are cross-currents in the tides of circumstance against which principles and men, no matter how strong they may be, are at times unable to make headway. These cross-currents may have their rise in great passions that cannot be stilled until they have run their course. It would be idle to assert that the atmosphere in which the Treaty of Versailles was made was free from enmity and vengeance; it would be transcending human nature if such were the case.

The treaty was made in the still smouldering

furnace of human passion. It could not have been otherwise. The memory of the millions of dead and wounded, of property and homes ruthlessly, wantonly, and methodically destroyed, and of the hideousness of the warfare but recently ended, made it necessary to face the impossibility of arriving at a fully ideal treaty. But steps are provided in the elastic mechanism of the Reparation Commission which will enable us, in the calmer days to come, to climb nearer to perfection.

I believe that every fair-minded man who can speak familiarly on the subject will agree that the repression and minimizing of the vengeful elements in the treaty were due in largest measure to Woodrow Wilson and the high purposes he set for ultimate attainment. The treaty may not embrace all he desired, but I believe that it embodies all that could have been obtained.

It is a fundamental mistake to assume that the treaty ends where it really begins. The signing of the document on June 28, 1919, at Versailles did not complete its history; it really began it. *The measure of its worth lies in the processes of its execution and the spirit in which it is carried out by all of the parties to the contract.*

It is true that the treaty is a severe treaty. The only question in dispute is: Does it embody the best attainable justice and wisdom?

I affirm that the problems presented at Paris which I here discuss were dealt with as effectively as possible at the time. If it were impossible to secure a treaty which was other than a human document, a method, however, was provided for removing later the obstacles that at Paris proved to be insurmountable. I am confident that in the Reparation Commission there was created a flexible instrument qualified to help effectuate a just and proper peace, if that desire and purpose be really present. When the world more fully and humanely understands and measures the problems in question, they can be soberly and wisely resolved.

If we so will it, there is that in the treaty which enables us to look forward with hope instead of backward with hate.

NOTE

It should be said that in the pages to follow I address myself only to those matters with which I was directly concerned in the making of the treaty. Where reference is made to the treaty, I have specifically in mind the reparation and economic sections.

It should be said further that I alone am responsible for the statements made in this volume.

HOW THE REPARATION CLAUSES WERE FORMED

For purposes of specific reference, the reparation and economic sections of the treaty, with marginal explanatory notes, have been reprinted verbatim at the back of this book. The reader will find the marginal notes of value in his scrutiny of the clauses. The marginal notes to the reparation clauses have been prepared especially for this volume. Those for the economic clauses appear substantially as they were written when the clauses were drawn. The notes to the economic clauses, particularly, illustrate the manner in which the Economic Commission kept itself informed as to the progress of its work.

I.

How the Reparation Clauses Were Formed.

At a plenary meeting of the Peace Conference held on the 25th of January, 1919, it was decided to apportion among various commissions the several subjects to be dealt with.

These commissions operated under the general direction of the Council of Ten composed of the chiefs of the delegations of the five principal Allied and Associated Powers and their Ministers of Foreign Affairs.[1]

Among the bodies thus established was the Commission on Reparation, which was charged by the Conference with examining into and reporting on (1) the amount which the enemy countries ought to pay by way of reparation; (2) what they were capable of paying, and (3) by what method, in what form, and within what time payment should be made.

The members of this commission and the nations which they represented were as follows:

United States of America:

Mr. Bernard M. Baruch, Chairman of the United States War Industries Board.

Mr. Norman H. Davis, Commissioner of Finance.

---

[1] Subsequently the Council of Ten was replaced by a Council of Four, composed of the heads of state of the United States, of Great Britain, of France, and of Italy. This Council was otherwise known as the Supreme Council or the Big Four.

Mr. Vance C. McCormick, Chairman of the War Trade Board.

Mr. Jerome Greene, Secretary.

British Empire:

The Rt. Hon. W. M. Hughes, Prime Minister of Australia.

The Rt. Hon. Lord Sumner of Ibstone, Lord of Appeal in Ordinary.

The Rt. Hon. Lord Cunliffe, Former Governor of the Bank of England.

Mr. Dudley Ward, of the British Treasury, Secretary.

France:

M. L. L. Klotz, Minister of Finance.

M. Loucheur, Minister of Industrial Reconstruction.

M. Albert Lebrun, Minister of Liberated Districts.

M. Cheysson, Inspector of Finances, Secretary.

Italy:

M. Salandra, Deputy, former President of the Ministerial Council.

M. Eugenio Chiesa, Deputy.

M. d'Amelio, Counselor of the Supreme Court.

M. Foberti, Chief of Section, Ministry of the Interior, Secretary.

Belgium:

M. Van den Heuvel, Minister of State.

M. Despret, Supreme Court; Director of the Bank of Brussels.

M. Bourquin, Professor at University of Brussels, Judicial Consul for the Ministry of Affairs, Secretary.

Greece:

M. Romanos, Special Envoy and Minister Plenipotentiary to Paris.

M. Michalacopoulos, Minister of State.

M. Speranza, Director of Ministry of Foreign Affairs, Secretary.

Poland:

M. Olchowski, Director of Department of War Indemnities at the Ministry of Finances.

M. Chamiec, Director of the National Loan Bank.

M. Zalewski, Secretary.

Portugal:

M. Egas Moniz, Minister of Foreign Affairs.[1]

M. Freire d'Andrade, Professor of the Faculty of Sciences, former Minister of Foreign Affairs.

M. Joao de Bianchi, Secretary.

Japan:

M. Kengo Mori, Financial Agent in the Japanese Embassy at London and Paris.

M. H. Nagaska, Councilor of the Japanese Embassy in Paris.

M. K. Tatsumi, Director of the Specio Bank of Yokohama.

M. K. Aoki, Secretary.

Rumania:

M. Danielopol, Envoy Extraordinary and Minister from the King to Washington; former Director of the National Bank of Rumania; former Deputy.

M. Zahariade, Civil Engineer, Inspector General, Assistant Director of Railroads, Member of Upper Board of Public Works.

M. Misu, Secretary.

Serbia:

M. Stoyanowitch, Deputy, former Minister.

M. Miloch Savtchitch, former Minister.

M. Drag-Doutschitch, Secretary.

Czechoslovak Republic:

M. Benes, Minister of Foreign Affairs.

M. Osuski, Chargé d'Affaires.

M. Slavick, Secretary.

---

[1]Replaced by Mr. Alfonso Costa, after the meeting of March 11, 1919.

Mr. Klotz, the French Minister of Finance, was chosen chairman of the commission and Mr. W. H. Hughes, Prime Minister of Australia and Mr. Van den Heuvel of Belgium, vice-chairmen.

The American representatives selected as their legal adviser John Foster Dulles, an international lawyer, who had had experience in several international conferences. Later on Thomas W. Lamont, a representative of the United States Treasury, was named as an alternate to Norman Davis. The American committee was assisted by a corps of experts, who had previously made an intensive field examination beginning immediately with the conclusion of the armistice. This group contained General McKinistry, Colonel Dillon, Leland L. Summers, and other engineers. They were assisted and advised by Prof. Allyn Young. Jerome D. Greene became the secretary of the American delegation and of the Interallied Reparation Secretariat.

The first meeting of the Commission on Reparation was held on Monday, February 3, 1919. It was then decided that the commission should proceed to consider the principles of reparation, and each of the nations represented on the commission was invited to file a statement of the principles as conceived by it.

The American reparation delegates approached their task with a fairly definite program. As to the actual physical damage wrought by Germany, their knowledge probably surpassed that of any other delegation. This was the result of field examinations which had been conducted by a number of the experts referred to above immediately at the conclusion of the armistice.

The American principles were based on pre-armistice negotiations as to what were to be the "terms of peace." President Wilson in his Fourteen Points had originally stipulated for healing acts to repair the structure and validity of international law and for the restoration of invaded areas. Before accepting these terms the Allies stated that by restoration they understood "that compensation will be made by Germany for all damage done to the civilian population of the Allies and their property by the aggression of Germany, by land, by sea, and from the air."

This interpretation had been accepted by the United States and by Germany. Accordingly, the American delegates prepared and filed with the reparation section of the Peace Conference a statement of reparation principles which involved:

(1) That Germany make good the damage resulting directly from acts clearly in violation of international law, such as the breach of the Treaty of Neutrality in favor of Belgium, illegal treatment of prisoners of war, etc.

(2) That Germany make good her pre-armistice agreement as to compensation for all damage to the civilian population and their property, this being construed by the American delegation to mean direct physical damage to property of non-military character and direct physical injury to civilians.

The American delegation was the only one to present any definite scheme of reparation. The other delegations merely filed general statements to the effect that the war being a wrongful act by Germany, Germany was responsible for all the loss and damage, direct and indirect, which resulted therefrom.

One of the Allies went even further and made claim for loss and damage resulting from the fact that the armistice was concluded so unexpectedly that the termination of hostilities involved it in financial losses. In no statement of principles other than that of the United States was any reference made to the pre-armistice negotiations as a foundation for, or limitation of, the Allies' rights to reparation.

The American program, as the most concrete and definite, at once became the basis of discussion. During several weeks of debate, it was subjected to the criticism of the other delegations, all of which, with the exception of the Belgian delegation, which was acquiescent, took strong exception to it.

Damage vs. War Costs.

The American contention was that we did not have a piece of plain, white, unscratched paper upon which to write the treaty, but that there already was written upon it, because of the acceptance of the Fourteen Points, a limitation which stated that only reparation of damage should be collected, and not the costs of the war.

The argument in favor of war costs was led by the British delegation, comprising Mr. Hughes,

Premier of Australia, Lord Sumner, and Lord Cunliffe. It was natural that the British should have vigorously supported the inclusion of war costs. Mr. Lloyd George had just been re-elected to power on a platform of collecting from Germany the costs of the war, "shilling for shilling, and ton for ton." The American program absolutely opposed this, and would have brought little reparation to the British dominions. That for Great Britain would have been limited to shipping losses and damages from aerial raids.

Although the attitude of Great Britain was thus quite natural, it was somewhat surprising that she was able to rally to her program France, Serbia, and other nations which had suffered substantial material damage. In accordance with the calculation of the American experts, the American program of reparations would have led to payments by Germany being apportioned among the Allied Powers somewhat as follows:

France	43 per cent.
British Empire	19 " "
[1]Belgium	24 " "
Italy	6 " "
Serbia	4 " "
Rumania	3 " "
Scattering	1 " "

Under the British scheme of inclusion of war costs, the proportion would have been somewhat as

[1]This relatively high percentage for Belgium is due to the exceptional position of Belgium as regards war costs which was provided for in the American program.

follows (the figures as a basis are very rough calculations, but will serve to illustrate the point):

France	24	per cent.
British Empire	40	" "
Belgium	1 7/10	" "
Italy	6	" "
Serbia	1 3/10	" "
United States	25	" "
Scattering	2	" "

It was obvious, therefore, that the American proposal was the more advantageous for the chief sufferers from the war unless Germany could pay a principal capital sum largely in excess of that required, in accordance with the American program, to make good actual physical damage, personal injury to civilians, etc. The Americans stressed the fact that Germany's capacity of payment could scarcely extend appreciably beyond that needed to meet the American program. Nevertheless the delegations of France, Serbia, and to an extent even of Belgium, did not openly espouse this program, which afforded them a particularly favorable position, chiefly because the program seemed to involve a sparing of Germany against which their public opinion revolted.

It is but fair to say that the arguments presented by the English and French delegations, which were more active than others, were based upon cogent reasons. The English contention, of course, was influenced by the mandate that had been given by their people in the election following the armistice. As a legal basis for this claim the British contended that they had agreed to make peace not merely on the President's Fourteen Points, but upon the principles enunciated in his subsequent addresses. They further contended that among these principles was the declaration that the settlement should be based on the justice of each item of the treaty.

Mr. Hughes in particular argued with force that the reparation clauses of the treaty would not be just unless they provided an adequate reparation for the heavy losses in blood and treasure which had been incurred by the British dominions, even though these dominions had been spared from actual physical destruction. He was earnestly supported by Lord Sumner, one of the recognized leading jurists of Great Britain. Both Mr. Hughes and Lord Sumner also likened the situation of Great Britain to that of Belgium, on the ground that Great Britain's war costs had resulted from Germany's breach of the Treaty of Neutrality of Belgium, to which treaty Great Britain was a party.

The French argument in favor of the inclusion of war costs was based on the terms of the signed armistice agreement of November 11, 1918. This agreement contained the following clause:

> Nineteen.—With the reservation that any future claims and demands of the Allies and the United States of America remain unaffected, the following financial conditions are required: Reparation for damage done.

This clause was followed by provisions respecting German public securities, Russian and Rumanian gold, etc. It was the French claim that this general reservation occurring subsequently to the discussions between the Allies, the United States, and Germany as to the terms of peace left the Allies free to present any claim for reparation which they saw fit.

In contending against these points the Americans urged that the specific declaration of the Allies relating particularly to the question of the amount of compensation to be paid by Germany was binding as against general statements contained in the President's addresses. These statements had not been definitely construed. They urged additionally that the pre-armistice negotiations as to the terms of peace which had been conducted by the heads of the Allied states were not subject to modification by the terms of the armistice agreement of November 11, 1918. The latter was a military document designed only to insure the Allies being in a position to enforce the peace arrangements previously entered into.

The texts of the opening and closing addresses of Mr. Dulles and addresses by Mr. Hughes and Mr. Klotz are contained in the addenda to this volume. A reading of the arguments will give an appreciation of the difficulties inherent in the solution of these problems, as well as of the vigor with which the conflicting viewpoints were urged.

The debate which the American program had evoked did in fact impress the other delegates. They could not, however, bring themselves to adopt this program. The American delegation thereupon proposed that the question of the inclusion of war costs be referred without prejudice to the Supreme Council. Mr. Hughes, earnest and sincere, fighting to the last for war costs, attempted to force a vote prior to this reference to the Supreme Council. He was confident that this would have shown the American delegation as a minority of one.

However, the motion for a vote was lost, and the matter was referred to the Supreme Council without a record of the decision of the delegations upon the question. After this action, taken in accordance with the American suggestion, the formulation of the reparation clauses of the treaty passed from the reparation section of the Peace Conference and became subject to the direct treatment of Mr. Wilson, Mr. Lloyd George, Mr. Clemenceau, and Mr. Orlando, with their several technical advisers.

President Wilson was on the ocean returning to America when the Supreme Council first took into its hands the problem of reparations. The American delegation had, however, presented to the President by wireless a full and impartial report of the divergent points of view. They requested his instructions as to whether they should persist in their original attitude with reference to war costs.

The President replied to the effect that the American delegation should dissent, and if necessary dissent publicly, from a procedure which "is clearly inconsistent with what we deliberately led the enemy to expect and cannot now honorably alter simply because we have the power."

Fortified by this vigorous support from the President, the American delegates, in informal conference, were able shortly to secure the acquiescence of Mr. Lloyd George, Mr. Clemenceau, and Mr. Orlando in the fundamental principle originally enunciated by the American delegation. This was that Germany's reparation obligations were to be determined in accordance with a fair construction of the Allies' pre-armistice declaration and that such construction excluded imposing upon Germany the "costs of the war," but was limited to what may be called actual damage.

There remained to be settled precisely what should be considered as damage as distinct from war costs. After considerable discussion and debate, the thirty-one categories of damage which had been reported by the Commission on Reparation were reduced to ten (see page 32). On these there was general agreement except as to pensions and separation allowances.[1] The inclusion of these items was vigorously urged by all the Allies, particularly Great Britain and France. With the abandonment of general war costs, these items afforded the only remaining basis for a large financial compensation from Germany for the tremendous sacrifices in blood and treasure which had been made by the British Empire. The French were insistent in

[1]By separation allowances is meant pay by the governments to families and relatives who normally depended for their support upon persons in military service.

view of the demands of their people that Germany should pay and thus relieve this sorely tried people, who have suffered more than the world probably will ever realize.[1]

Unless the French delegates were firmly convinced of Germany's ability to pay considerably in excess of a capital sum of $15,000,000,000, it is difficult to understand their acceptance of the inclusion of pensions and separation allowances in the categories which Germany had to pay. It was forcibly brought to their attention that probably Germany could not pay much more than a capital sum of $15,000,000,000. Hence, if pensions and separation allowances were included in the bill *pari-passu* with the other categories, France would not receive so large an amount as if these items were left out.

Without pensions and separation allowances, the bill against Germany was estimated to be approximately $15,000,000,000, which it was generally thought she could pay. France would have received full payment for her devastated areas. With the inclusion of pensions and separation allowances without a priority for the devastated areas, France would have a larger bill to present, but

---

[1]My first-hand observations of the unnecessary destruction in Belgium and France has convinced me that the devastated areas of Belgium, France, Italy, Poland, Serbia and Rumania should receive preferred consideration. The loss of cattle to a peasant means at least as much to him as does the loss of a ship to a great merchant.

would receive a less sum of money than if she had excluded these items. On the other hand, England and her dominions would get more.

Sooner or later, if the amount of Germany's indebtedness is fixed at about a capital sum of $15,000,000,000, France must insist either upon a priority for her devastated areas or a larger percentage than her claims under the categories would entitle her to; otherwise she will lose out.

There was a division among the American delegation which made it frankly hesitant between maintaining on the one hand its original strict and possibly legalistic construction of the pre-armistice declaration (which would have excluded pensions and separation allowances), and supporting on the other hand a liberal construction which would admit the right of compensation for damage to the homes and families behind the front as well as damage to the houses at the front.

Some advanced the principle that financial loss resulting from the absence of a wage earner did not cause any more "damage to the civilian population" than did an equal financial loss involved in the payment of taxes to provide military equipment and like war costs. On the other hand, it would not be easy to meet the contention that Germany should be liable for compensation not merely for damage to the buildings upon which civilians depended for housing, but also for injury or loss of life of those upon whom the civilians depended for support. Payment for a destroyed chimney was not to be placed above compensation for a lost life or a pension for a blinded or wounded soldier.

In addition, it was argued that the inclusion of these terms would not increase the amount which Germany would pay. Her debit without them would amount to all that she could pay as a capital sum. It was urged that it merely changed the proportion of the distribution of collections among the Allies on what seemed to them to be a more equitable and satisfactory basis.

The final argument that won the unanimous approval of what was known as the Big Four was a memorandum submitted by General Smuts. He, as is well known, was one of the most liberal and courageous men at the Peace Conference. This memorandum read as follows:

NOTE ON REPARATION.

The extent to which reparation can be claimed from Germany depends in the main on the meaning of the last reservation made by the Allies in their note to President Wilson, November, 1918. That reservation was agreed to by President Wilson and accepted by the German Government in the armistice negotiations, and was in the following terms:

> "Further, in the conditions of peace laid down in his address to Congress on January 8, 1918, the President declared that invaded territories must be restored, as well as evacuated and made free. The Allied Governments feel that no doubt ought to be allowed to exist as to what this provision implies. By it they understand that compensation will be made by Germany for all damage done to the civilian population of the

> Allies and to their property by the aggression of Germany by land, by sea, and from the air."

In this reservation, a careful distinction must be made between the quotation from the President, which refers to the evacuation and restoration of the invaded territories, and the implication which the Allies find in that quotation and which they proceed to enunciate as a principle of general applicability. The Allies found in the President's provision for restoration of the invaded territories a general principle implied of far-reaching scope. This principle is that of compensation for all damage to the civilian population of the Allies in their persons or property, which resulted from the German aggression, and whether done on land or sea or from the air. By accepting this comprehensive principle (as the German Government did), they acknowledged their liability to compensation for all damage to the civilian population or their property wherever and however arising, so long as it was the result of German aggression. The President's limitation to restoration of the invaded territories only of some of the Allies was clearly abandoned.

The next question, is how to understand the phrase "civilian population" in the above reservation, and it can be most conveniently answered by an illustration. A shopkeeper in a village in northern France lost his shop through enemy bombardment, and was himself badly wounded. He would be entitled as one of the civilian population to compensation for the loss of his property and for his personal disablement. He subsequently recovered completely, was called up for military service, and after being badly wounded and spending some time in the hospitals was discharged as permanently unfit. The expense he was to the French Government during this period as a soldier (his pay and maintenance, his uniform, rifle, ammunition, his keep in the hospital, etc.) was not damage to a civilian, but military loss to his Government, and it is therefore arguable that the French Government cannot recover compensation for such expense under the above reservation. His wife, however, was, during this period, deprived of her bread-winner, and she therefore suffered damage as a member of the civilian population, for which she would be entitled to compensation. In other words, the separation allowances paid to her and her children during this period by the French Government would have to be made good by the German Government, as the compensation which the allowances represent was their liability. After the soldier's discharge as unfit, he rejoins the civilian population, and as for the future he cannot (in whole or in part) earn his own livelihood, he is suffering damage as a member of the civilian population, for which the German Government are again liable to make compensation. In other words, the pension for disablement which he draws from the French Government is really a liability of the German Government, which they must under the above reservation make good to the French Government. It could not be argued that as he was disabled while a soldier he does not suffer damage as a civilian after his discharge if he is unfit to do his ordinary work. He does literally suffer as civilian after his discharge, and his pension is intended to make good this damage, and is therefore a liability of the German Government. If he had been killed in active service, his wife as a civilian would have been totally deprived of her bread-winner, and would be entitled to compensation. In other words, the pension she would draw from the French Government would really be a liability of the German Government under the above reservation, and would have to be made good by them to the French Government.

The plain, common-sense construction of the reservation therefore leads to the conclusion that, while direct war expenditure (such as the pay and equipment of soldiers, the cost of rifles, guns, and ordinance and all similar expenditures) could perhaps not be recovered from the Germans, yet disablement pensions to discharged soldiers, or pensions to widows and orphans, or separation allowances paid to their wives and children during the period of their military service are all items representing compensation to members of the civilian population for damage sustained by them, for which the German Government are liable. What was spent by the Allied Governments on the soldier himself, or on the mechanical appliances of war, might perhaps not be recoverable from the German Government under the reservation, as not being in any plain and direct sense damage to the civilian population. But what was, or is, spent on the citizen before he became a soldier or after he has ceased to be a soldier or at any time on his family, represents compensation for damage done to civilians and must be made good by the German Government under any fair interpretation of the above reservation. This includes all war pensions and separation allowances, which the German Government are liable to make good, in addition to reparation or compensation for all damage done to property of the Allied peoples.

(Signed) J. C. Smuts.

Paris, March 31, 1919.

Categories.

It thus having been decided to include pensions and separation allowances, the categories of damage for which Germany is held responsible were finally formulated as follows:

Compensation may be claimed from Germany under Article 232 above in respect of the total damage under the following categories:

(1) Damage to injured persons and to surviving dependents by personal injury to or death of civilians caused by acts of war, including bombardments or other attacks on land, on sea, or from the air, and all the direct consequences thereof, and of all operations of war by the two groups of belligerents wherever arising.

(2) Damage caused by Germany or her allies to civilian victims of acts of cruelty, violence or maltreatment (including injuries to life or health as a consequence of imprisonment, deportation, internment or evacuation, of exposure at sea or of being forced to labour), wherever arising, and to the surviving dependents of such victims.

(3) Damage caused by Germany or her allies in their own territory or in occupied or invaded territory to civilian victims of all acts injurious to health or capacity to work, or to honour, as well as to the surviving dependents of such victims.

(4) Damage caused by any kind of maltreatment of prisoners of war.

(5) As damage caused to the people of the Allied and Associated Powers, all pensions and compensation in the nature of pensions to naval and military victims of war (including members of the air force), whether mutilated, wounded, sick or invalided, and to the dependents of such victims, the amount due to the Allied and Associated Governments being calculated for each of them as being the capitalized cost of such pensions and compensation at the date of the coming into force of the present Treaty on the basis of the scales in force in France at such date.

(6) The cost of assistance by the Government of the Allied and Associated Powers to prisoners of war and to their families and dependents.

(7) Allowances by the Governments of the Allied and Associated Powers to the families and dependents of mobilised person or persons serving with the forces, the amount due to them for each calendar year in which hostilities occurred being calculated for each Government on the basis of the average scale for such payments in force in France during that year.

(8) Damage caused to civilians by being forced by Germany or her allies to labour without just remuneration.

(9) Damage in respect of all property wherever situated belonging to any of the Allied or Associated States or their nationals, with the exception of naval and military works or materials, which has been carried off, seized, injured or destroyed by the acts of Germany, or her allies on land, on sea or from the air, or damage directly in consequence of hostilities or of any operations of war.

(10) Damage in the form of levies, fines and other similar exceptions imposed by Germany or her allies upon the civilian population.

Special Provisions For Belgium.

There remained, as a question of principle, the special position for Belgium which the American memorandum had originally proposed. All of the principal Allied and Associated Powers, having accepted the view that their own claims to recovery of war costs should be renounced, were reluctant to admit an exceptional position for Belgium—a position which, however sound in international law, would be difficult to explain to their own people. The American experts had filed with the Supreme Council a formal reservation of the rights of Belgium as construed by the United States. The representatives of Belgium were encouraged by American sympathy and by the stand of the President. They finally secured provisions for compensating Belgium for the entire loss to which she had been subjected as a result of Germany's violation of the Treaty of Neutrality.

A further special measure in aid of Belgium was

adopted at the same time. The general principle accepted by the Allied and Associated Powers was that they would share in Germany's reparation payments in proportion to their allowed claims. To permit the immediate restoration of Belgium it was, however, felt equitable to accord to Belgium a certain priority in time of payment. An arrangement was accordingly entered into whereby Belgium will receive, on account of the reparation payments to which she is entitled, the equivalent of 2,500,000,000 gold francs, as preferred payment out of the first cash, securities, and deliveries in kind received from Germany pursuant to the Treaty of Peace.

A final principle of major importance was that of "joint and several liability." It was urged by some that each of the Allies should look exclusively to reparation from that enemy country with which it had chiefly been in military opposition. This would have meant, in effect, that Italy, Serbia, Greece, and Rumania would have had to secure their reparation exclusively from the Austro-Hungarian Empire, which was so dismembered and in so critical a financial condition that hope of reparation from this source was highly problematical. These nations under the leadership of Italy therefore regarded it as of great importance that this principle should be established: that all of the assets of the enemy states should be pooled into one fund and that all of the Allied and Associated states should share in this fund in proportion to their approved claims. This latter principle, which was fully concurred in by the American delegation, was ultimately accepted.[1]

The conditions of peace thus took concrete form with the reparation principles formulated in general accord with those which the American delegation had originally proposed. These principles are found in the following articles of the treaty:

Article 231, recognizing Germany's moral responsibility for the war and its consequences.

Article 232, providing for Germany's obligation to make compensation in accordance with the pre-armistice declaration.

Article 232 (third paragraph), providing for special compensation for Belgium for war expenses resulting from the violation of her neutrality.

With the settlement of the principles of reparation, consideration was given to the scarcely less important question of the methods of its performance. The problem presented itself in three main aspects:

First, restitution of objects removed but still in being; second, reparation in kind of property destroyed; third, financial restitution.

Restitution is provided for wherever objects have been taken away and are capable of identification. Where cash has been taken away or seized, restitution of an equivalent amount can be required without the necessity of identifying the exact coin or paper currency which has been seized; such identi-

---

[1]Reparation payments made by Austria, Hungary, and Bulgaria are to go into the general reparation fund.

fication being in the nature of the case practically impossible.

Because of world shortages of the articles necessary to permit effective reparation, direct reparation in kind from Germany was thought of paramount importance where money alone would not suffice to restore the injured party to his pre-war position.

Ships.

With regard to ships, there was general agreement that practically all of Germany's merchant marine should be surrendered as part replacement of the losses caused by German submarine activities. The question of the allocation of these ships among the different Allied and Associated Powers proved one of the troublesome problems of the Conference. It is here briefly described as typical of the divergence in national points of view which almost every economic problem presented, and the solution of which was made possible only by mutual concession and appreciation of the position of the others.

The French proposed to allocate to the Allied and Associated Powers in proportion to their respective war losses, and to place in a pool for that purpose, all ships which on August 1, 1914, flew the German flag. This would have resulted in the pooling of all ships condemned by prize court (chiefly British) and ships seized in the Western Hemisphere (chiefly by the United States and Brazil).

The British proposed the pooling of all ships which on the date of the coming into force of the treaty were entitled to fly the German flag. This, in British opinion, would have pooled ships seized by the United States, Brazil, Cuba, etc., without prize-court decisions, and would have left undisturbed the title to ships which had been passed through the prize court.

The American delegates proposed that title to all German ships seized during the war should be confirmed in the captor nation, and that only the remaining German ships be placed in the pool.[1]

Mr. Lloyd George strongly urged that ships, which were at most only useful additions to the economic resources of other nations, constituted the very life blood of the British Empire. He protested the injustice of a principle that, in one case, would permit a nation which had not been an active belligerent to increase its tonnage nearly tenfold while only five per cent. of Great Britain's tonnage losses would be replaced.

Mr. Clemenceau urged the claims of France as being in a financial situation which rendered it exceedingly burdensome for her to pay foreign charter hire for her imports. He pointed out that

1German shipping taken over by the United States during the war should not be confused with German shipping surrendered to the Allies under Armistice Agreements for use in the repatriation of troops and for relief purposes. Certain of these latter ships, including the IMPERATOR, were temporarily allocated to the United States for operation and subsequently were returned by the United States.

during the war France had abandoned ship construction so as to devote herself exclusively to other forms of war activities to which her industries were better adapted.

President Wilson declined to accede to any proposition that would involve the surrender by the United States of ships which had been taken over by act of Congress.

A suggested solution was that the United States should retain all vessels seized by her; but this action was not to be extended to other nations of the Western Hemisphere. It was not possible, however, that the United States, despite its far greater contribution to the war, should accept a more favored position than that accorded to her Pan-American associates, who to some extent had entered the war under the inspiration of and as an expression of sympathy towards the United States.

The problem was finally solved by agreeing to place all the belligerents on an equality. The right was recognized to retain seized German tonnage upon the condition that payment be made for reparation account up to the fair value of ships retained in excess of those apportioned to replace war losses.

Coal.

Owing to generally decreased production, and in part to the destruction of the war, the world's coal situation was so acute that reparation in the form of coal deliveries was considered of great importance. Though Germany might pay in money or in manufactured goods, France feared that without assured deliveries of coal, she would find her furnaces idle, her workmen unemployed, and her industrial reconstruction delayed. This depended in great measure on the repair of the Lens coal fields, which had been destroyed with such a deliberation and thoroughness that five years will hardly suffice to restore them.

The first coal demand upon Germany is thus for the delivery to France annually for ten years of an amount of coal equal to the difference between the current production and the pre-war production of the destroyed French mines. This amount is not to exceed 20,000,000 tons per annum for the first five years and 8,000,000 tons per annum for the succeeding five years. France, on her part, undertakes to exercise due diligence in repairing the mines. Germany herself has been given the opportunity to make proposals whereby her own engineers will repair the mines as a credit on Germany's reparation account. As the mines are gradually restored to normal operations, the deliveries on this account will diminish and may cease entirely before the expiration of the contract.

The second series of coal demands is subordinate to the first and of a different character. France, Belgium, and Italy have always been largely dependent upon German exports of coal. These nations felt a real and quite understandable apprehension. It was that this dependence might in future be utilized by Germany to extort economic concessions, which in effect would largely nullify the reparation and economic terms of the treaty.

Accordingly, as a second category of coal provisions, France and Belgium are given an option upon German coal up to the normal pre-war exports of Germany to those countries, and provision is made for Italy's necessities. These options can only be exercised in the event that the Reparation Commission considers that their exercise will not unduly disturb the economic life of Germany. That is, if Germany has coal for export, she must export it to these countries rather than to others. The price of the coal to France, Belgium, and Italy is to be the same as that charged to German citizens.

There is much misunderstanding regarding the coal clauses. As stated above, the Reparation Commission can authorize under the treaty (Part VIII, Annex 5, Paragraph 10) the postponement or cancellation of deliveries, if it considers that the full exercise of the options would interfere unduly with the industrial requirements of Germany.

There is a great fallacy prevailing as to the production and distribution of raw materials in the world. Only in time of war and blockade are the location and ownership of coal or other raw materials important. At all other times the producer desires to sell to those who can use his raw material. The principal supply of cotton in the world is in the Southern states, yet great mills have been built for the manufacture of cotton goods in Europe. Rubber and tin are produced outside the limits of the United States, Germany, and France, and yet great factories are built in those countries for their use.

It will be found that the French who demanded and the Germans who objected to the coal clauses were unnecessarily alarmed. *When normality in production of coal in Germany and Europe returns, the producer will find the most available market for coal where it had previously existed. This will take place only when that section of Europe containing coal gets back to work. This is largely within the hands of the Germans themselves.*

The following statement from a résumé of Herr Karl F. Von Siemens, chairman of the Siemens & Halske Company of Berlin, on the industrial situation in Germany, is illuminating and interesting in this matter:

> The chairman, proceeding to discuss the economic life of the country, stated that it is too frequently asserted that this is dependent upon other countries and that the Germans will soon come into swing again if they can again obtain the necessary raw materials from abroad. In his opinion this argument may be correct in regard to one or two industries, but it is not the case with many of them, and in these instances the decline is just as great as in those which need foreign materials. The principal thing lacking is coal, not because the Germans have lost too much coal, or have to make deliveries to their late enemies, but because an insufficient quantity of coal is produced as compared with former peace times, and cannot be distributed among consumers.

The coal provisions are therefore of a negative rather than positive character, designed to prevent Germany from exercising economic pressure upon France, Belgium, and Italy by arbitrarily withholding the normal movements of her coal to these nations. The option granted by the treaty upon a portion of German chemicals and dyestuffs is similar, and transitory in character and purpose, lasting for only five years.

When Europe stops fighting and gets back to work there will be no shortage of coal or other necessities of life.

Reconstruction Material.

To expedite the reconstruction of the devastated areas, it was held advisable to require Germany to deliver construction material such as wood, cement, brick, certain types of machinery, etc. This right can be exercised only under very carefully drawn restrictions and through the medium of the Reparation Commission. To the commission is reserved the right, after examining lists of desired articles which must be prepared within a short period of time, to decide whether the demand shall be forwarded to Germany as one which Germany can meet without undue injury to German economic life. In no event shall deliveries extend for more than four years. The Reparation Commission has further to take into account whether the desired materials can be secured elsewhere in the world's markets under equally advantageous conditions as to price and time of delivery.

Cattle.

The devastated areas had been completely denuded of live stock, which had been driven away or consumed by the armies of occupation. Estimates furnished by the German Government showed that the live stock of Germany was little, if any, numerically inferior to the pre-war supply. There had been, to be sure, a considerable decrease in the weight of cattle and in the quantity of milk production. This resulted from the shortage in Germany of suitable cattle-feed. It was lack of food for cattle rather than lack of cattle that was the limiting factor in the production of milk and meat in Germany. The food situation of Germany would not be appreciably affected by a small reduction in the numbers of live stock. It was thus apparent that it would be entirely equitable to replace in France, Belgium, or Italy a small percentage of the pre-war live stock of the devastated areas, by deliveries in kind from Germany.

The justice of the foregoing provisions for reparation in kind was suggested on the ground of the economic ruthlessness with which Germany prosecuted the war. The reparation delegates were presented with convincing evidence that the German armies had systematically destroyed industrial property with no military reason, but for the sole purpose of rendering the Allied states unable to resume their economic life after the war. Wherever possible, and in preference to destruction, the Germans actually carried away, for installation in Germany, important units of machinery. The same procedure had been followed with regard to live stock, which had been either consumed or driven back into Germany; and the fine-blooded cattle and horses of northern France and Belgium had been advertised for sale and for breeding purposes in Germany.

The provisions of the treaty for reparation in kind will operate only partially to make good the results of this destructive economic warfare prosecuted by Germany.

How Much Should Germany Pay?

While the most immediate and satisfactory form of reparation is reparation in kind, obviously only a relatively small proportion of "categories of damage" could be compensated for in this way. These categories of damage, which Germany was to be obligated to meet under the terms of the treaty, are the basis from which will be figured or assessed the amount of Germany's indebtedness, credit being given for reparation in kind.

The greater part of reparation, particularly after the first two or three years, would necessarily take the form of money payments or bonds. The question of the amounts, periods, and method of payment to be required of Germany proved, perhaps, the most troublesome single problem of the Peace Conference. The committee to deal with this subject was among the first to be appointed and the last to make its report.

The first thought, and a perfectly proper one, that occurs is, Why was not a fixed sum determined and settled in the Treaty of Peace? The American contingent contended all the way through for a fixed and reasonable sum. Their reasons were that it was better for all concerned to have a definite amount. It was well for the Allies so that they would know exactly what they could depend upon to aid in the rehabilitation of their own financial and economic life, and it was well for Germany and the other debtor nations to know what they had to pay, so that they could set about paying it. While all might have agreed that a fixed sum should be determined within the limit of Germany's ability to pay, many difficulties appeared.

No one knew how much Germany owed. No one yet knows how much Germany owes. No one knew how much Germany could pay. No one yet knows how much Germany can pay. There was a wide divergence among the Allied experts as to what Germany could pay. The amounts discussed varied from $8,000,000,000 to $120,000,000,000, both extremes, singularly, being of English origin. One of the difficulties in the situation was that a certain great English financial expert asserted with confidence that Germany could pay the latter figure. The amount of damages under the treaty categories was estimated by various delegates at from $25,000,000,000 to several times that sum.

Another obstacle in the way of fixing a definite sum was the unwillingness of the various delegations to present official estimates of the amount of their damage. During meeting after meeting of the first sub-committee of the Commission on Reparation, the American delegates urged and pleaded for figures of damages. They recognized that no precisely accurate figures could then, if ever, be given. There were, however, methods of computation available which could be trusted to give approximately accurate results. The American delegates themselves had such estimates not only for the United States, but for other nations. The figures were based on the field examinations and studies made by American experts. But while each nation sought access to these American estimates as a guide to the damage suffered by other nations, no nation was willing to accept the American estimate as applicable to itself.

The British delegation was disposed to support the American delegation in its efforts to secure definite figures and itself finally filed a provisional estimate of British losses. The French remained obdurate to the end and refused to make any estimate of their losses, on the ground that at that time such estimates would be only guess-work, and that the least conscientious guesser would be the greatest gainer.

Finally, the American delegation took the position that it could not consent to demanding any fixed sum from Germany unless satisfied of damage to at least that amount.

The refusal of most of the Allies to introduce any evidence of their own on this point or to accept the American estimates was, therefore, one of the compelling reasons leading to the postponement of fixing the amount of the German indemnity to a time when the amount of damage could be more scientifically estimated. The American delegates could with difficulty resist giving opportunity for scientific and careful estimation and checking of each nation's claims. It was fairly obvious that such claims would exceed Germany's ability to pay, yet the precise accuracy of each claim was none the less of great practical moment. This was the more true, since these claims were then expected to constitute the basis upon which each nation was to share in the payments that Germany makes.

The situation was further complicated by the attitude of the peoples of the nations involved. They demanded the uttermost farthing from Germany under the categories, on the theory that their burdens should not be made heavier to themselves and lighter to Germany. Germany in 1870 had been enabled to extract from France $1,000,000,000, an amount then not dreamed possible of payment. Germany, had in a short period of time, grasped such a large share of the world's trade as to create a perhaps exaggerated impression of her commercial and financial powers and recuperative ability. These facts made even the most conservative pause in determining the amount within her ability to pay. Indeed, there was divergence of opinion even among delegations as to the amount that Germany could pay.

Many doubted the wisdom of collecting too large an amount because of the adverse effect it might have upon the creditor nations, and argued along the following line:

Obviously only a relatively small portion of Germany's debt could be paid out of her then existing resources. The limit of her resources was agreed upon to be not more than $5,000,000,000, including ships, credits, etc. From this amount was to be subtracted the payment for the armies of occupation and amounts necessary for food and raw materials for Germany's rehabilitation. Further payments would have to be earned by the performance of services for the rest of the world in the form primarily of exports.

The amount of reparation thus becomes the measure of service which the world is willing that Germany should render to it. Large reparations could be paid only under conditions whereby the world affords Germany every encouragement to render to the balance of the world more service than the balance of the world renders to Germany. It further implies that the Allied and Associated Powers will force the German people to surpass their own in modesty of living, in industry, and in productive energy. Qualities which every Allied Government would desire to inculcate into their own people would be adopted by the German people, thanks to the external coercion which the Allied and Associated Powers would be threatening.

Germany would become the workshop of the world. Not only would the world's market be opened to the goods made in Germany, but the economic life of the world would necessarily adjust itself to the dependence upon German service. Once the reparation period were passed, it would be impossible for the economic fabric of the world at once to be readjusted to independence of that service upon which it had long become dependent. Trade would continue to move in its accustomed channels. Now, however, Germany's excess of service to the world would be at a price, with the result that the value of service rendered by Germany as reparation during the next generation would, in large part, be recovered by Germany in succeeding generations, and Germany would dominate the economic movement of the world.

In the unanimous report of the reparations section of the Peace Conference, it is stated that large reparation payments will require that Germany "turn herself into a nation of exporters organized for the purpose of paying the reparation claims of the Associated Governments, * * * The development by the enemy countries of such a policy as just described may lead to the creation, especially in Germany, of an organization so highly developed and so skillful as to be calculated in the future to have considerable and perhaps unfavorable influence upon the markets of the world."[1]

While the force of the foregoing observations appealed in principle to some, it was natural that the various Allied and Associated Powers should have different practical reactions. France, burdened with debts, with great industrial areas blasted, with man power shattered, was concerned primarily with securing relief during the next generation. In the face of immediate financial and economic problems of extreme gravity, the specter of German economic supremacy thirty years hence did not appear alarming, particularly as France herself had never been a dominant factor in international trade.

This attitude of France was largely shared by Italy and Serbia. Belgium, however, was apparently more apprehensive of the danger of forcing

[1]It was also brought forward that a crushing policy would precipitate an exodus of Germans and a consequent Germanizing of Poland, Russia and the Balkans. This would result in a greater future danger for the Allies than even the menace just passed. A hopelessly burdened Germany, with the attendant social reflexes, was not a pleasant picture for her neighbors and the world in general to contemplate.

Germany to organize into a great industrial machine. Great Britain should logically have been even more apprehensive, as being less dependent upon relief from Germany and as desirous herself to play the principal role of manufacturer and broker for the world. The English were, however, reluctant frankly to adopt a policy of moderate reparation, which, however much in the real interest of Great Britain, would have involved a direct repudiation of election pledges.

The United States, while directly involved to a relatively small amount, was interested from the standpoint of stabilizing world conditions. If it is to be a recipient of German reparation payments, it will be only to a comparatively small extent. *But unquestionably the industrial and financial development of the whole world for a long time to come will be largely influenced by the reparation settlement.*

The Americans continually brought forward the necessity of fixing a definite sum.[1] They urged the necessity of doing so because of the needs of the Allies themselves. They urged that money given now and expended would be of greater value than a larger sum received later. They urged the crying need of all the Allied peoples for rehabilitation and readjustment, and the necessity for this purpose of a new basis of credit. What they had in

[1]In an endeavor to compromise the different views, an unsuccessful effort was made to fix more definite terms by arranging for a minimum and maximum sum.

mind was the preservation of the economic structure and the saving of Europe from bankruptcy.

The President and his financial advisers passed days and weeks vainly endeavoring to convince their colleagues in the Allied and Associated Governments that it was impossible for Germany to pay anything like the sums required under the categories. They further submitted that even if this were possible, the Allied Governments could not afford, and would in time recognize that it was not to their advantage, to exact payments that could be made only at the expense of their own trade. *Therefore, in the American view it was to the interest of the Allied and Associated Governments to fix a reasonable, definite amount that Germany could pay and that they could afford to have her pay.*

It is pertinent to point out that at the time in question it was intimated in one quarter that if insistence were made on fixing a definite amount before the Allies had a chance to present their claims and to study and know more fully the ability of Germany to pay—a sum which might prove later on to be less than Germany could pay—the Allies might be in a position where they could put forth the following claim:

> If you ask us to lessen our claims upon Germany for indemnity, which she admits she owes, what will you do for the loan made to us for the prosecution of a war which was as much your war as our war, the amount of which clearly exceeds our ability to pay unless we are allowed to get the last possible dollar out of Germany?

Of course, it was generally recognized that the indebtedness of the Allies to the United States had no relation to Germany's reparation obligations to the Allies. As a matter of fact, the economic and financial recovery of the Allies, and hence their ability to pay America, would be increased rather than diminished by reducing and fixing Germany's debt at an amount which could be paid and which could be capitalized as a means of obtaining funds therefrom for immediate reconstruction purposes.

It is interesting to observe that one of the foremost critics of the treaty and of the President's position upon it, and the one, perhaps, who advocates the smallest fixed sum for Germany to pay which has been seriously urged, couples his argument with a provision that the United States shall cancel the entire indebtedness due her from the Allies. Not only so, but he suggested that the United States shall also be guarantor of a new series of bonds to be issued for the rehabilitation of Europe.

To expect that these problems could receive any wise final solution at the Peace Conference itself discloses a visionary confidence that ignores the complexity of the questions and the difficulty of the conditions under which the peace negotiators had to labor.

The world demanded and was entitled to expect a prompt formulation of conditions of peace. Final solution of the reparation clauses necessarily had to be deferred. The difficulties were accentuated by the need of securing acceptance of the reparation solution by the affected nations that were to be signatories to the treaty. All of these nations were interested in reparations from varying points of view.

Furthermore, reparations had become a leading popular and political issue among the European allies. The white heat of war had not yet had time to cool. Reparation was popularly regarded as a measure of moral retribution rather than as an index of future trade movements. This popular feeling could not but influence the peace delegates.

One must be either ignorant, vicious, or an impractical idealist to contend that in the foregoing circumstances it was humanly possible to have found at the Peace Conference a sound, definitive solution of the German reparation problem which would have met with ratification.[1] No one man or group of men is responsible for the conditions which created this situation; they inhered in the character of the war itself and in the war's aftermath.

The American delegates realized at last the insurmountable obstacles to fixing at that time a reasonable amount of reparation. Thus they came to the conclusion that they should not assume the responsibility of objecting to an effort by the Allies

---

[1]Ever since the signing of the treaty the Allies have been seeking a specific solution, yet without definite success. This will come only after time has helped to cool passions, when calm judgment prevails, and when Germany fully realizes that she must meet her obligations.

to collect from Germany what she owed them, provided they would agree to certain safeguards against the dangers of such a course.

The United States, relatively speaking, had no great direct interest in what Germany was to pay, but she had a sincere desire for all nations concerned that the world should not be thrown into disorder and its commerce deranged by an attempt to create and collect a debt which could not be paid.

Because of misrepresentations and misconceptions as to the amount that Germany could pay and as to the amounts which she owed, it was impossible to agree upon an amount to be exacted from her. What she *could* pay was in any event less than the amount that she *should* pay. The American delegates, therefore, consented reluctantly to the present arrangement. That arrangement is by no means, however, what it is represented to be by the critics, for it offers decided safeguards that they fail to mention.

The Peace Conference accordingly adopted a provisional solution of the question of the amounts to be paid by Germany in succeeding years. The experts of the Allied and Associated Powers were in substantial agreement that the quick, realizable surplus assets of Germany amounted to about $5,000,000,000. This figure was accordingly adopted to measure the values which Germany must surrender by May 1, 1921.

The value of reparation in kind—namely, ships, coal, reconstruction material, etc.,—made prior to this date, is accounted as a credit toward the sum.

The sum is likewise inclusive of amounts to be paid by Germany toward the expenses of the armies of occupation. Further flexibility is given to this particular reparation clause. It is in the power of the Reparation Commission to permit Germany to deduct from the $5,000,000,000 the necessary funds to pay for such food and raw materials as the Reparation Commission deems necessary to be imported into Germany.

The question of further payments by Germany is left unsettled, but with a direction that it be determined by May 1, 1921. The power to fix this amount is vested in the Reparation Commission. To this commission the Peace Conference sought to give those attributes that the Peace Conference itself had lacked but which were recognized as essential to an intelligent solution of the reparation problem.

The Reparation Commission.

The character and powers of the Reparation Commission may be outlined as follows:

(1) The Reparation Commission is compact in character. Provision is made for five delegates to be named respectively by Great Britain, France, Italy, the United States, and Belgium, the latter, when shipping matters are under discussion, being replaced by Japan, and when Austrian, Hungarian, and Bulgarian questions are being considered, replaced by the Kingdom of the Serbs, Croats, and Slovenes. The commission is thus from the standpoint of membership a practicable and workable body.

(2) The Reparation Commission is invested with broad power. It is appointed as agent of all the Allied and Asso-

ciated Powers for the purpose of collecting reparations, and is given general control and handling of the entire reparation problem. In particular it has the power to fix the amount of reparation for which Germany is liable. Possibly the most unusual power which the commission possesses is that of interpreting conclusively the reparation provisions of the treaty. The commission may thus override technical difficulties and inconsistencies of expression. Indeed, it is invited to treat the reparation clauses of the treaty in a practical business-like way with disregard, if need be, of legal and diplomatic technicalities.

(3) The Reparation Commission is afforded time to study maturely the problems upon which it must pass, although, on the other hand, it must act with reasonable diligence. By May 1, 1921, when Germany's first installment has been paid, the Reparation Commission must have determined the amounts, dates, and methods of future payments. Even this solution may, however, be subsequently adjusted if events should prove it to be unworkable.

Decisions of the Reparation Commission are not "revisions" of the treaty. Any such revision would require resubmission of the treaty and its approval by new parliamentary ratifications. The decisions of the Reparation Commission are executory without action by any government, except in the case of reducing or canceling the amount of the debt or of certain postponements.

The general power and discretion vested in the Reparation Commission cannot, however, be exercised arbitrarily. Certain fundamental principles are established for the guidance of the Reparation Commission.

The first, and perhaps the most important, of these principles, is that reparation is to be collected with due regard to the economic life of Germany. One of the weightiest matters that confronted the Peace Conference was whether the Allied right to reparations should be used to destroy Germany economically.

Obviously such destruction would of itself limit the amount of reparation obtainable. One cannot eat his cake and have it too. But there were many who preferred to see Germany crippled economically even at the expense of future reparations. This view did not prevail, and one of the reiterated instructions to the Reparation Commission is that it shall have due regard for the economic life of Germany. The coal options are to be enforced only with regard to the industrial needs of Germany (Par. 10, Annex V). Reconstruction material is to be demanded only in relation to the industrial life of Germany (Par. 4, Annex IV). In their interpretive note to Germany of June 16, 1919, the Allied and Associated Powers made the following declaration:

> The resumption of German industry involves access by the German people to food supplies, and by the German manufacturers to the necessary raw materials and provision for their transport to Germany from over-seas. The resumption of German industry is an interest of the Allied and Associated Powers, as well as an interest of Germany. They are fully alive to this fact and therefore declare that they will not withhold from Germany commercial facilities without which this resumption cannot take place, but that, subject to conditions and within limits, which cannot be laid down in advance, and subject also to the necessity for having due regard for the special economic situation created for

Allied and Associated countries by German aggression and the war, they are prepared to afford to Germany facilities in these directions for the common good.

The foregoing declaration contemplated in particular the temporary retention by Germany of certain ships to carry essential imports until new German construction could meet this need.

Before passing on any question involving Germany's capacity of payment, the Reparation Commission is required to give Germany adequate opportunity to be heard (Par. 9, Annex II). The only defaults by Germany which subject her to penalty and retaliatory action are wilful defaults (Par. 18, Annex II, and Article 430).

A second great guiding principle established as an instruction to the Reparation Commission is that the performance of reparation by Germany should be limited to the period of one generation—*i. e.*, thirty years from May 1, 1921.

It may be true that the financial burdens of the war cannot be liquidated in one generation. Nevertheless, these financial burdens differ radically from reparation obligations that might involve a certain subjection to foreign control. It did not seem either equitable or wise to extend the latter type of obligation beyond the period of the generation which could be charged with a share in the moral responsibility of the war.

From a practical standpoint, the present capital values of a sum payable without interest after thirty years is very small. To have required interest payments on sums due after thirty years would have meant the practical impossibility of ever discharging the principal of the debt.

The essential spirit underlying the reparation settlements is thus aptly described in the following sentences from the Allied and Associated note to Germany above referred to:

> The vast extent and manifold character of the damage caused to the Allied and Associated Powers in consequence of the war has created a reparation problem of extraordinary magnitude and complexity, only to be solved by a continuing body, limited in personnel and invested with broad powers to deal with the problem in relation to the general economic situation. The Allied and Associated Powers, recognizing this situation, themselves delegate power and authority to a Reparation Commission. This Reparation Commission is, however, instructed by the treaty itself so to exercise and interpret its powers as to insure, in the interest of all, an early and complete discharge by Germany of her reparation obligations. It is also instructed to take into account the true maintenance of the social, economic, and financial structure of a Germany earnestly striving to exercise her full power to repair the loss and damage she has caused.

A careful analysis can but sustain the above quotation. It is frequently asserted that the reparation clauses are "impossible" of performance. Such statement is fallacious, because it is provided that any demonstrated incapacity of execution in itself excuses lack of performance. *As noted, no penalty is stipulated except for the execution of those obligations which Germany can, but wilfully refuses, to perform.*

There is not an important reparation demand made upon Germany which cannot be adjusted under the treaty to meet Germany's needs and capacity. It is true that this creates a régime of some uncertainty, entailing economic disadvantages. The machinery, however, is established whereby this uncertainty can and should be rapidly dissipated under conditions far more conducive to a wise settlement than those which prevailed during the first four months of 1919.

Unfriendly critics charge that the Reparation Commission will be an instrument of oppression. That is the extreme German view.[1] The American delegates who took part in the drafting of the reparation clauses believe that the representatives of the other nations who participated in preparing the reparation settlement meant to be just. The Americans are convinced that in the execution of the reparation clauses justice and wisdom will prevail. Interests both selfish and humane will demand this outcome.

German Bonds.

While the ultimate amount to be paid by Germany was thus left to the judgment of the Reparation Commission, the Allies desired to have in their hands certain evidences of indebtedness issued by

---

[1]It is claimed that Germany and future generations of Germans will have to bear a great burden. This is true, and it is justly true. While Germany should not be put to impossible tasks, her burden certainly should be no less, but logically and in justice should be greater than that of the nations and peoples whom she has wronged.

Germany. Such evidence might be available for realization for some immediate credit, and would correspond roughly with the provisional estimates as to Germany's capacity to pay. The bonds representing this evidence could not be put into circulation until the Reparation Commission unanimously so determined. It was accordingly provided that Germany upon the coming into force of the treaty should issue to the Reparation Commission certain bonds. These bonds are of four issues.

The first is an issue of 20,000,000,000 gold marks payable May 1, 1921, without interest. These bonds correspond to and will be discharged in part by the $5,000,000,000 (20,000,000,000 gold marks), which as above described was fixed as the amount that it was estimated Germany should be able to raise in the immediate future principally out of accumulated assets. Of this $5,000,000,000, part might be used to pay for the expenses of the armies of occupation, and part for essential food and raw material imports. But it is stipulated that if the initial payment does not suffice to discharge the full 20,000,000,000 marks of bonds due May 1, 1921, the balance shall be carried forward and converted into bonds of a later (the third) series due in 1951.

The second issue of bonds is to cover the war costs of Belgium. The amount of these bonds has not been definitely fixed, but it will be about 4,000,000,000 gold marks to fall due on May 1, 1926.

The third series of bonds is to the amount of 40,000,000,000 gold marks ($10,000,000,000) bearing interest at $2\frac{1}{2}$ per cent. from 1921 to 1926 and 5 per cent. thereafter with 1 per cent. for amortization. This, it was estimated, would retire the bonds in about 1951 or in the thirty-year period fixed as the period for Germany's reparation obligations.

There is a contingent agreement to issue a fourth series of bonds for another installment of 40,000,000,000 gold marks. These bonds, however, cannot be issued until the Reparation Commission is satisfied that Germany can meet the interest and sinking fund obligations on this and on the second and third series of bonds.

Further issues by way of acknowledgment and security may be made as the commission subsequently determines from time to time.

Additional safeguards are thrown around these bond issues by the provision that it requires the unanimous consent of the Reparation Commission to determine the amount and conditions of bonds or other obligations to be issued by the German Government. The same consent is required to fix the time and manner for selling, negotiating, and distributing such bonds.

It is sometimes asserted that by these bond provisions the treaty has already fixed an amount to be paid by Germany that is beyond her capacity, and that thus the treaty is "impossible of fulfillment" and must be "revised." This contention ignores many essential facts. The aggregate of bonds to be delivered without further affirmative action of the Reparation Commission is about

$16,000,000,000. Of this sum, $5,000,000,000, or as much of this sum as possible, is to be discharged by the initial payment and by various credits provided for by the treaty. This would leave $11,000,000,000 of bonded indebtedness plus whatever part of the $5,000,000,000 is not discharged as stated above.

These bonds are delivered to the Reparation Commission merely as "security and acknowledgment" for the payment of the amount which will ultimately be fixed. Without unanimous action of the Reparation Commission, they cannot be negotiated or distributed. They in no sense involve a final pre-judgment of the amount Germany will in the end be called upon to pay. Even if they did, the amount is subject to cancellation or diminution.[1] Irrespective of these bond provisions, the amount of Germany's liability remains open for fixation in accordance with the cooler judgment of the Governments represented in the Reparation Commission.

The German Attitude Toward Reparation.

The reparation clauses were in substantially the form that has been described when the treaty was handed to the German peace delegation, which was given the opportunity to present its observations thereon. The German comments, which were very lengthy, were de-

[1] This requires the unanimous consent of the Governments represented on the Reparation Commission.

voted in large part to criticism of the supposed excessive and inquisitorial powers of the Reparation Commission. The reply did, however, contain an express recognition of Germany's willingness to assume all damage and war costs that had fallen upon Belgium as a result of the violation of Belgium's neutrality. It also contained Germany's recognition of obligation to make good the devastation caused in France. The Germans further made a definite proposal for fixing the amount of their liability. The sum proposed by Germany was 100, 000,000,000 gold marks payable without interest. Of this sum 20,000,000,000 marks was to be paid by May 1, 1926. But against this sum Germany demanded as credits not merely the items which were provided as credits in the conditions of peace, but also the value of war material delivered under the armistice terms, the value of public property in ceded territory, and a proportionate part of the German public debt (including war debt), which could be attributed to ceded territory.

The remaining 80,000,000,000 marks would be paid thereafter in annuities, not exceeding 1,000,-000,000 gold marks per annum for the first ten years. At the end of ten years the amount of annuities was to be arrived at by a mutual agreement. This German offer as a whole was further conditioned on Germany receiving certain concessions in respect of other economic terms of the treaty.

The American delegates recognized that the German offer as made could scarcely be regarded as satisfactory, particularly on account of the numerous credits and conditions that Germany demanded. It was likewise unsatisfactory because of the low amount of the annuities suggested, which would have deferred final payment for many years, and thus greatly reduce the present capital value of the sum offered. The Americans did feel, however, that the German offer was sufficiently substantial to afford hope that some satisfactory, definite sum might be arrived at. Accordingly, the American delegation, with the authorization of the President, again renewed its efforts to induce the Allies to fix by the treaty the final amount which Germany would be required to pay, and it again presented the arguments showing the advisability and wisdom of such action.[1]

With reference to the German counter-proposal concerning reparation, the following verbatim memorandum shows the line of reasoning of the American delegation at that time and the arguments presented to the conferees:

June 3, 1919.

(1) The German counter-proposal offering, subject to various credits, payments to aggregate 100 milliards of

[1]The Americans, with the approval of the President, made an effort to arrange a meeting with the German economic advisers for the purpose of discussing reparational and economic matters. In this effort they were supported generally by the economic and business advisers of the various governments. The military advisers almost without exception were opposed to this meeting. But it was impossible to obtain the unanimous support of the leaders of state.

marks gold, raises the question of whether a determined effort should not again be made to fix Germany's reparation liability in terms of definite figures.

(2) The American reparation delegates have always been unanimous in the belief that the treaty should fix a definite sum for Germany to pay. The considerations advanced by the German reply in favor of a fixed sum are not new in themselves, but are reinforced by a comprehension, daily becoming clearer, of the critical financial situation of Europe.

(3) There have been but two principal arguments against the fixation of a definite sum—namely:

(a) It is impossible to tell today just how much Germany might be able to pay within the next generation. A miscalculation might release Germany, at heavy cost to the Allies, from a just liability which, it would subsequently develop, Germany was fully capable of discharging. Germany's liability should, therefore, be expressed elastically, so as to insure the utilization of Germany's full future capacity of payment to make good the almost unlimited damage caused by her.

(b) The political situation among the Allies is so unsettled, and the popular expectation of relief by payments from Germany runs so high, that it might have serious political consequences to name definitely Germany's liability. Even the highest figure which has been considered would disappoint popular expectations.

(4) With respect to the latter argument, it may be observed that the financial and economic situation of Europe is so serious that no government would adopt, merely as a matter of domestic politics, a policy which is not defensible on its merits. The only political consequences to be taken into account are those relating to the stability of government in general. It is conceivable that a severe popular

disillusionment at this time might lead to social unrest, which would have really serious national and international consequences. It seems far more probable that to continue to perpetuate uncertainty as to the amount of Germany's payments will merely postpone an awakening until a time when the situation may be even more critical. In the intervening period the people will not have exerted their fullest efforts to aid themselves, as would have been the case had they earlier realized their real situation.

(5) With regard to the argument that there is danger today of underestimating Germany's capacity to pay, it may be said that this risk is perfectly real and fully recognized. It is, however, a risk which must be balanced against the risk of attempting to secure from Germany more than she can pay, or adopting a procedure which destroys Germany's incentive to pay. Of the two risks the latter is infinitely the more serious. To seek too much jeopardizes the whole; to obtain too little involves only the loss of the difference between what is, and what might have been, paid.

(6) It is further to be observed that what the world requires, and requires immediately, is a new basis of credit. A dollar today is probably worth two dollars five years from now. A definite obligation assumed by Germany, under conditions which warrant us in believing that Germany herself has the will and believes she has capacity to discharge such obligation, will serve as an immediate basis of credit. A far larger amount assumed under equally satisfactory conditions eighteen months from now would not begin to have the same practical value. Also a larger amount imposed today at the point of the bayonet and in the face of declarations by Germany (which will be accepted by conservative persons throughout the world) that the sum is far in excess of her capacity, would prove of little or no value as a basis of credit.

(7) The present reparation plan is, in our opinion, open to the serious objection that it may, in practice, operate to

destroy economic incentive on the part of the present generation in Germany. Germany is set a task without end, and the more she labors the more will be taken from her. Furthermore, little is obtainable under the plan in the immediate future, aside from deliveries of bonds, which will not command the confidence of investors because, among other things, they may be followed by an indefinite amount of similar bonds. And it will be in the interests of Germany herself to destroy popular confidence in the initial installments of bonds taken from her, as once these bonds acquire any marketable value, still further issues will be taken from Germany.

(8) Europe's need is immediate. Any substantial delay in securing from Germany an obligation having a substantial present value may involve consequences which will approach a disaster. The risks involved in delay far outweigh the difference between such definite sum as might be fixed today and the most optimistic estimates which have been made as to Germany's capacity.

(9) We therefore strongly recommend that the opportunity offered by Germany's counter-proposal be taken advantage of to fix a definite obligation which Germany will assume in a manner at least semi-voluntary. The German people can then be left free from the continuing interference and control of the Reparation Commission to work out their own problem in their own way. Under such conditions there is every reason to believe that the German people will again become a stabilizing, productive, and constructive factor in the world's economy.

(10) To secure acceptance by Germany of a high figure, it may be necessary to leave Germany a certain amount of working capital and sufficient shipping to meet her domestic requirements. This, in principle, we are prepared to recommend.

At one time it appeared as if the American efforts would come to a successful termination.[1] But although some changes were made in other sections of the treaty as a result of the German reply, a sudden fear seized some of the Allies that too great changes might be brought about. The Americans were, therefore, unable to make the reparations more definite. Every other delegation solidly and stolidly refused to move. If at that time there was one apparently unanimous opinion among the delegates of the Allied and Associated Powers, it was that the reparation clauses should stand as made. They felt that they had already made a tremendous concession in limiting their claims to reparation in such a way as to exclude war costs. To fix a sum before examination of the facts was to them like giving Germany a quit-claim in the dark.

Where questions of principle were involved, and particularly the conditions of the pre-armistice agreements, the American delegation, under the leadership of President Wilson, could and did take

---

[1]The American delegation was particularly encouraged as the result of a conference of the members of the British cabinet called by the Prime Minister to consider the German reply. It is understood that some of the cabinet members were inclined to make changes in various parts of the Treaty along the line of the American contention. Some changes were made, but the support expected by the Americans for the fixing of a definite sum was not forthcoming. Obviously, certain present-day critics have either not been in possession of these facts or, possessing them, have misinterpreted them.

a definite position. It refused to make compromises which would have involved a departure from a fair construction of the pre-armistice terms. Once, however, these questions of principle had been settled, and the basis for determining Germany's debt had been fairly arrived at, the question of letting Germany off with less than she owed was a matter of expediency and not of principle. In this question the final word necessarily had to rest with the creditor nations, of which the United States was not one of outstanding importance, so far as financial claims were concerned.

The most that the American delegation could do was to urge upon its associates, in their own and in the whole world's interest, the necessity and practical wisdom of fixing Germany's liability. When, however, they were not persuaded, the American delegation felt that it had done all that it properly could do in the circumstances. To have adopted any other course and to have insisted as a matter of right that creditors of Germany should waive in part their admittedly just claims against Germany might have encouraged the effort to re-open the whole question of Interallied indebtedness and refinancing.

I refer here to the proposition brought forward to the effect that bonds for part of the reparations to the value of £1,800,000,000 ($9,000,000,000) as from January 1, 1925 (the date from which they bear interest), should be issued by enemy states or by certain states acquiring enemy territory. The proposition further provided that these bonds should be guaranteed by the principal Allied and Associated Governments, by the three Scandinavian Governments, and by the Governments of Holland and Switzerland.

It was proposed under this scheme that the United States should guarantee 20 per cent. of the issue. In the event of any of the guarantor Governments failing to meet their guarantees, the remaining guarantor Governments might be obligated to double their original proportionate share. That might have made it necessary for the United States to guarantee 40 per cent., or about $3,450,000,000. No serious consideration was ever given to this plan. But it is evidence of an attitude on the part of others which would have been strengthened if through our insistence a fixed definite sum had been made before the Allies had had an opportunity to examine all of the matters and had come to the conclusion of the necessity in their own interest of fixing this definite sum. While these arguments may not have been tenable, it can easily be perceived that they might have been embarrassing.

The conditions of peace, in so far as they related to reparations, were not modified as a result of the German observations. The Allied reply contented itself with explaining a number of points with reference to the powers of the Reparation Commission, which had been misunderstood by the Germans. It was thought by the American delegation that the elastic provisions in the reparation clauses afforded instrumentality whereby, when the world came to a liberal view of its situation, a definite, reasonable sum could be arrived at which would be to the advantage of the creditor nations.

This view is being justified by the various conferences that have been and are now (July, 1920), taking place, at which discussions have been and are revolving around the fixing of a definite sum. Belief in the elasticity of the coal clauses has been justified by the action taken modifying the deliveries of coal to meet the situation.

Doubtless, any one of the Allied and Associated nations might itself have negotiated a separate treaty with Germany, which to the nation concerned would be more satisfactory than the treaty actually signed. It should be borne in mind, however, that the immediate and grave danger that faced the world after the conclusion of the armistice with Germany and that faced all those at the Peace Conference was that the twenty-seven nations comprising the Allied and Associated Powers could not agree among themselves.

The present relation between Italy and the Kingdom of the Serbs, Croats, and Slovenes with regard to Fiume illustrates how readily the Allied and Associated Powers might have become broken among themselves. If, estranged from one another, they had left the Peace Conference without an agreed basis for their future relations, an appalling situation would have resulted, and a period of world-wide chaos would have been inaugurated.

An important date in the history of the world is

May 7, 1919, when the Allied and Associated Powers finally agreed among themselves on the conditions of the future peace. This agreement was reached and a solution found only through a spirit of mutual concession. History will judge whether the leaders who made the necessary concessions were wise and had a just appreciation of international values. For each nation to have insisted upon a treaty which embodied exclusively its own ideals and promoted exclusively its own national interests would have involved separate and conflicting treaties of peace. This would have divided the world into many hostile camps and precluded any harmonious co-operation in the scheme of reparation and in the rehabilitation of the world.

* * * * * * *

This volume goes to press as the Allies have concluded a conference with the Germans at Spa. The deliberations there showed the impossibility of having arrived at a perfect solution of reparations in the Paris conference. It is becoming increasingly plain that the reparation clauses were framed to make possible a successful future solution of the problems involved.

As the needs of the Allies are better understood, as Germany's ability to pay is more definitely disclosed, as her willingness to meet her obligations is increasingly manifested, and, above all, as the anger and hatred engendered by the war cool, a wiser solution becomes possible. The final outcome must carry with it the sanction of a public opinion awakened to the needs of the world. The machinery of the Reparation Commission awaits this aroused opinion.

DRAWING THE ECONOMIC CLAUSES

II.

Drawing the Economic Clauses.

The outbreak of the war disrupted all business and all social relations between nationals[1] of the belligerent states. One of the problems with which the Peace Conference had to deal was the re-establishment of these relations on a satisfactory basis.

The framers of the economic clauses were faced with the same conditions and enshrouded in the same atmosphere that I have endeavored to depict in the opening pages of this book. Each nation, with its destroyed or crippled business, felt that it was entitled to special treatment in order that it should be placed in a position to carry its burdens and take its former place in the world's trade. Practically the whole industrial life of the Allies had been converted from a peace to a war footing. To convert it back from war to peace and to re-establish financial arrangements and trade routes would require time.

In addition, the Allies saw in front of them a Germany with machinery and factories intact and ready immediately to get into competition for the world's market. The unfair trade practices of Germany had sunk deeply into the minds and hearts of the Allies, who were determined that, at least for a transition period, until they were able to get on their feet, these practices should not be renewed.

---

[1] A general term meaning citizens or subjects.

The Allied delegations particularly and forcibly alleged that the German differential or discriminatory tariff had been used as a definite weapon of commercial aggression and that in discussions in Germany respecting the tariff it was often referred to as a means of imposing Germany's will upon other nations. Furthermore, they asserted that Germany had so quickly mastered such a large share of the world's trade that there was a great danger to the Allies that if Germany were left free to use her previous methods, they would soon be economically crushed unless at least a temporary relief was given from the use of such methods.

It was with much difficulty that the Allies were convinced against their desire and what they believed to be the necessity of placing permanent and very severe restrictions upon Germans and German trade. In the end, however, the restrictions or prohibitions that were imposed are only temporary and transitory, are no real hardship upon Germany, and are justifiable in all the circumstances.

In passing it may be said that it was always the Americans who had to take the lead in arguing against extreme measures. As can be imagined, this was by no means an agreeable position. Any apparent restrictions are in no sense a measure of the original demands. Repeatedly it had to be brought to the attention of all concerned that a crippling of the industries of Germany would prevent the payment of any large sum of reparation and was contrary to the spirit of the terms set for peace. But at all times one was forcibly struck with the spirit of fairness and conciliation of the various delegations. There was a general desire to give up as far as possible for the common good what appeared to each delegation to be just and necessary demands. Many subjects in dispute were left to the decision of the American representatives.

At an early stage of the conference the Economic Drafting Committee, composed of one representative of each of the five great Powers, was appointed for the purpose of recommending to the conference economic measures for incorporation into the treaty.

This task, while perhaps less conspicuous than that entrusted to the Reparation Commission, was probably of equal importance. It embraced the work of laying the foundations for the renewal of private business and public and private intercourse generally between the two sets of enemy countries. The stipulations ultimately framed for this purpose doubtless affect directly a larger number of persons in the activities of their daily lives than do any other provisions of the treaty. They are concerned with private business and private property rights of nationals of the belligerent countries and with commercial and social relations and treaty arrangements to which these countries were parties before the war.

The Economic Drafting Committee was composed of Mr. Bernard M. Baruch, representing the United States; Mr. Georges Clementel, Minister of Commerce of France; Sir Hubert Llewellyn Smith, permanent secretary of the British Board of Trade;

Mr. Crespi, representing Italy; and Mr. Kenejo Tatsumi, representing Japan.

The committee divided its discussion under two broad heads:

First, that of transitory measures covering a period of rehabilitation following the war; and, second, that of the re-establishment of relations broken off by the outbreak of the war.

The subject of transitory measures involved not alone temporary prohibitions against discriminatory practices of Germany, but the question of the allocation among nations of raw material for a short period until the former belligerent countries could have an opportunity to readjust themselves. Proposals concerning these measures were based in large part upon the so-called Paris Economic Conference, which had looked forward to an economic alliance among the Allies and a boycott of Germany after the war had closed. The United States, of course, was not a party to the Paris Economic Conference, and at the time the intent of this conference was not concurred in by America.

The discussion of transitory measures contemplated among other things a division of raw materials by the interested nations. The American representative soon convinced the others that so far as the United States was concerned the development of such a scheme was not practicable and was at variance with the terms of the armistice. He made clear in particular the obstacles of dealing with domestic questions of this kind which were, so far as the United States was concerned, matters peculiarly within the province of Congress. As being indicative of the possible attitude of Congress, he called attention to its action at an earlier date in refusing to grant a credit of $1,500,000,000 for the purchase of raw materials in America for the benefit of Allied countries.

The French particularly were very insistent upon the adoption of the proposed transitory measures and urged them vigorously, not only before the drafting commission and the economic commission, but also before the Supreme Economic Council. While the position of the several countries was appreciated, the American representatives in all three of these bodies took an unequivocal stand against these proposals, except with regard to certain measures for food relief. They felt that the action advocated should be undertaken through private rather than through public instrumentalities.

Another question which was discussed to some extent was the advisability of limiting the amount of materials that might be permitted to go into Germany as compared with other countries. The idea underlying suggestions with respect to this matter was to give the Allied and Associated countries for a temporary period an advantage over Germany in the supply of raw materials. Proposals of this kind were opposed by the American and other representatives on the ground that an economic war should not be conducted against Germany after the conclusion of peace. Such proposals, apart from their being regarded as wrong in principle, of course would necessitate negotiations respecting questions involving matters of domestic concern and would require Congressional action for their consummation.

With reference to the subject of economic cooperation, it is only fair to state the position of some of the delegations in order to show the conditions which were forcing them to ask for such co-operation which they felt in all justice they were entitled to.

There had been great industrial co-operation during the war. This was becoming more definite and more perfected as the war went on. Not alone was there a single command in the field and on the sea, but we were gradually headed toward a central command, under American leadership, of the strategy behind the line controlling the material resources of the world, of which there was continuing mobilization for the purposes of the war. This mobilization of the industrial resources of the world achieved such good results that the Allies believed the co-operation should be continued for a period of readjustment and rehabilitation.

There is very little general knowledge of the extent to which this great industrial co-ordination had taken place. Not alone had there been a mobilization of the resources of America, but the United States and the Allies in their efforts to obtain success in the war had reached beyond their own borders. Through international co-operation they were commencing to control the production, allocation, and prices of many things throughout the world, even of those things not produced within their own territories. This control was working so smoothly and to such general satisfaction that the Allies desired its continuation at least for a short period of reconstruction.

The American representative contended that the control should end with the war, and that with peace there should be a restoration of personal initiative. As a matter of fact such control could not be continued without special Congressional legislation, to which the American representatives thought Congress and American producers would very properly be opposed. The control that had been in effect during the war was more or less voluntary, and born of the need of the hour.

The following is the substance of a brief general statement by a French representative of the French position with regard to the necessity of economic relief and co-operation:

> It was not only a part of France that was devastated, but the whole, for the whole of France had been turned over to war purposes. There was a lack of stability in France that had been brought about by a state of war for four and a half years. One tenth of the territory of France had been invaded by the enemy and destroyed, this being the region wherein lay the deposits of iron, coal, etc. France was obliged to import many times as much as she formerly did. All of her exports had been suppressed and no distinction could be made between France's devastated areas and France as a whole. The entire country had been thrown out of joint by the war.

An extemporaneous statement of an Italian representative is so illuminating that its substance is given below:

To my mind the most important point is the restoration of the economic régime, and this is a question that we must discuss first. Italy is now in a very serious condition. We had a debt at the end of December of 65,000,000,000 lire, and this will be increased by next December to 90,000,000,000. The wealth of Italy was calculated during the war at 80,000,000,000 and after the war at 120,000,000,000 lire, or $24,000,000,000; and so we calculate we shall have a debt at the end of next December equal to three-fourths of our national wealth.

If we reckon what the financial burden on the Italian people will be, we must figure first this debt of $18,000,000,000, on which there will be interest and amortization charges, the latter at 2 or 3 per cent.; a general taxation of 7 to 8 milliard lire; the general running expenses of the country amounting to 5,000,000,000 lire—altogether we shall have a general taxation of 12,000,000,000 to 13,000,000,000 lire or $2,500,000,000. In this case each Italian would have to pay a lira of taxation per day. The average wage of an Italian during the war was 2½ lire per day. If you take children, women, and old people who do not work, you may state that during the war the earning capacity of the average Italian was 2 lire per day. Then each Italian will have to pay a tax of a lira a day, which is exactly one-half of his earnings. Suppose that the wages double, it will still be an unbearable taxation; for if the earnings go up, so will the expenses, since everything will cost more.

So the restoration of the economic system is for Italy a question of life or death, and we think it must be done in two ways: We must restore our commercial balance—that is, the balance between imports and exports—and we must restore what we call the contributing capacity. We must have a system under which each Italian will be able to pay the tax to defray the general expenses as well as the debts of the country. We have been expending during the war, in the last years especially, six times the amount of money which we received from our exports; in other words, the amount of our imports has during the last year been six or seven times greater than our exports. So our debt is growing enormously, and it will still grow enormously. We are still now importing six times as much as we actually export, because our industrial export has been cut to nothing, has been so destroyed by the war that we view the future with great anxiety.

On the other hand, the contributing capacity is so low that we must find some way to reduce the taxation on the people, or some way to increase their earnings. So you can see that Italy cannot recover if this unhappy condition is permitted to continue. If the preliminary policy is not settled, we shall be not a free but a weak, contributor state, economically speaking.

I need not remind you that Italy, having fought with all her energy and having given nearly all of her wealth for the war, is altogether a devastated country. From our viewpoint we cannot see that only the northern part of Italy has been devastated. It is all devastated. What the enemy has not devastated, the staggering taxes have. Therefore how is it possible for a country that has given so much of its wealth to come into any agreement under such desperate conditions? I quite expect that you will consider this tragic condition of Italy. We are prepared to do our best, but before we can you must give us the great help required.

The Economic Drafting Committee submitted a report to the Supreme Council, whereupon the so-called Economic Commission was organized for the purpose of framing stipulations to deal with subjects which had been considered by the committee as proper for incorporation into the treaty. Thomas W. Lamont and myself were designated

American members of the commission. Realizing the scope and technical nature of the work that would be involved, I had previously called to my assistance in my capacity as the American representative on the Economic Drafting Committee, the following gentlemen because of their expert knowledge of the subjects to be considered:

Dr. Frank W. Taussig, then chairman of the United States Tariff Commission; Alex Legge, vice-chairman of the United States War Industries Board and general manager of the International Harvester Company, which has business establishments in every important country of the world; Leland L. Summers, a mechanical engineer of an international reputation, who had been the technical adviser of the War Industries Board and who possessed a knowledge of English, French, and German manufacturing processes; Charles H. MacDowell, formerly head of the Chemical Division of the United States War Industries Board; Fred K. Nielsen, who is now the solicitor for the Department of State; Bradley W. Palmer, of Boston, who had been sent to Paris by the Alien Property Custodian, for whom he had acted as counsel; John C. Pennie, of New York, a noted expert in international and American patent law; and J. Bailey Brown, of Pittsburgh, an expert in patents, trade-marks, and copyrights. Prof. Allyn Young, already attached to the Peace Commission, served as an alternate for Mr. Lamont.

The following countries were originally given representation on the Economic Commission: The

United States, the British Empire, France, Italy, Japan, Belgium, Brazil, China, Poland, Portugal, Rumania, and Serbia.

The work of the commission was apportioned among sub-commissions, which presented their conclusions to the commission for its action. The report of the full commission was finally submitted to the Supreme Council for its consideration substantially in the form in which the Economic Clauses appear in the text of the treaty.

Part X of the treaty, designated Economic Clauses, comprises provisions in which the United States has a more direct and permanent interest than in any others, aside from the Covenant of the League of Nations. These provisions are concerned largely with technical subjects that enter into international relations. Such subjects were dealt with by men possessing the necessary technical training. However, these stipulations are readily comprehended by the lay mind from the standpoint of their general purport and are discussed briefly from that standpoint.

The so-called Economic Clauses of the treaty are not "impossible" of performance, as we sometimes hear it said of the economic provisions of the treaty generally. Nor can it correctly be said that they are unjustly onerous upon Germany. Nor are they in derogation of the letter or the spirit of any of President Wilson's Fourteen Points.

The several subdivisions of this interesting part of the treaty entitled Economic Clauses are designated as follows:

(1) Commercial Relations; (2) Treaties; (3) Debts; (4) Property, Rights, and Interests; (5) Contracts, Prescriptions, Judgments; (6) Mixed Arbitral Tribunal; (7) Industrial Property. The comprehensive nature of the articles embraced by these designations is indicated by a mere enumeration of them.

Commercial Relations.

Among the most important provisions under the general classification of Commercial Relations are those pertaining to German customs duties and the regulation of questions relating to exports and imports generally. The salient features of these stipulations, which are found in Articles 264 to 270, may be briefly indicated.

A temporary maximum rate of duty of six months' duration on imports from the Allied and Associated Powers is prescribed—namely, the most favorable duties applied to imports on July 31, 1914. This provision applies for a further period of thirty months to certain commodities, respecting which special agreements with Allied and Associated Powers existed before the war, in addition to certain products which, it seems, found an exclusive or almost exclusive market in Germany before the war. Certain temporary tariff concessions are secured to products shipped into Germany from Luxemburg, and from territories ceded to France and Poland. Most-favored-nation treatment in matters relating to tariffs and laws and regulations with regard to prohibition pertaining to exports and imports is secured to the Allied and Associated Powers for a period of five years. The general nature of these stipulations may be briefly indicated.

No great severity appears to be involved in the requirement imposed on Germany to maintain for a period of six months the most favorable rates of customs duties which were in force for imports into Germany on July 31, 1914. And there seems to be no reason to question the sincerity of those nations, some of them sorely ravaged by war, which insisted that the economic situation in their countries made a definite German tariff for a temporary period highly important to them; that such a period was necessary in order to avoid serious economic disturbance by a sudden change of tariff. At the end of this brief period Germany will be free to alter her rates. Probably at least six months' time to effect a readjustment will be required.

For a period of five years from the coming into force of the treaty, products which originate and come from Alsace and Lorraine are exempted from payment of customs duties on importation into Germany up to the average amount sent annually into Germany from 1911 to 1913.[1] Similar conces-

[1]At the end of the Franco-Prussian war, similar arrangements were made for the admission into France of goods originating in Alsace-Lorraine. The duration of such arrangements was shorter than that provided in the Treaty of Versailles, due to the fact that the industries of Alsace-Lorraine in 1871 were much less specialized than they are today, and required less time for readjustment.

sions are made to Poland, with respect to territory ceded to her, for a period of three years, and for five years to Luxemburg, which has for a long time enjoyed the benefits of the German Customs Union.

The Germans do not appear to have found seriously objectionable these provisions having for their purpose the temporary protection of these territories during a transition period, so that the latter may not be abruptly deprived of their former markets, which had previously existed through German channels.

The provisions securing the application, for the period of three years, to imports of certain products from Allied and Associated countries of the most favorable rates of the German tariff which were in force in 1914, have a similar purpose. Certain products, the output of which in countries bordering on Germany was especially adjusted to German needs, are by these provisions temporarily assured of markets enjoyed before the war.

By stipulations in the nature of the so-called favored nation clauses found in the usual commercial treaties, Germany is forbidden to discriminate against the Allied and Associated Powers in matters relating to imports and exports. She is obliged to adhere for a period of five years to a non-discriminatory régime, such as obtains at present under the laws of the United States and, I believe, under the laws of England and not a few of the Allied and Associated countries. By a number of treaties she was bound to adhere to such a régime before the war. Treaties of this character were wiped out in the Treaty of Peace so far as the Allied and Associated Powers were concerned. The treaty affords a temporary substitute arrangement with regard to foreign trade relations. It is difficult to perceive any harshness in this arrangement.

Summarizing the general effect of stipulations in the treaty relating to the foreign commerce, it appears that Germany exercises full sovereign rights over imports and exports, subject only to the transitory requirement that all of the Allied and Associated Powers must be treated on a footing of absolute equality among themselves and with other foreign countries, and to certain temporary limitations respecting gold exports and respecting the fixed customs duties and the temporary concessions to which I have called attention.

Germany might prohibit all exportation or importation. She can make partial prohibitions, but such prohibitions must not be discriminatory against any of the Allied and Associated Powers as compared with any other foreign country during this temporary and transitory period. And she is free to fix any tariff rates subject to the temporary limitations just mentioned.

It is of particular importance to such countries as Poland, Serbia, Italy, and France, which have suffered so greatly from the war, that Germany shall be restrained for a temporary period from employing any methods of commercial discrimination against them. Doubtless it can be confidently hoped that at the end of such a limited period the economic disturbances resulting from the war will be so adjusted and the passions engendered by the war so allayed as to permit the conclusion of reasonably satisfactory commercial arrangements between the various belligerent countries.

Mention may be made in this connection of Articles 323 and 327, which refer to commercial relations, but which are found in a section of the treaty under a different designation. They secure national and most-favored-nation treatment to vessels of the Allied and Associated Powers with respect to cargoes carried by them, shipping charges, and regulations of various kinds.[1]

Articles 274 and 275 have for their purpose the protection of nationals of the Allied and Associated countries against unfair trade practices in Germany. The German Government is required to adopt appropriate measures to protect the produce or manufacture of any of the Allied and Associated Powers from all forms of unfair competition in commercial transactions. It is obligated to prevent the importation, exportation, manufacture, distribution, sale, or offering for sale in German territory of all goods bearing upon themselves descriptions or marks which have a tendency to convey, directly or indirectly, a false indication of the origin, type, nature, or special characteristics of such goods.

---

[1]These articles are limited in their unilateral form to a five-year period. At the end of the five years they apply only to such of the Allies as give reciprocal privilege.

Economic Sections of the Treaty

A section of the treaty, embracing Articles 276 to 279, contains a number of important provisions in the nature, broadly speaking, of those found in commercial treaties. These provisions secure to nationals of each of the contracting countries the right to do business in the other, unhampered by discrimination in matters of taxation and of property regulations of various sorts.

Article 278 in this section of the treaty seems to have some exceptional interest to the United States, in view of our large alien immigration, and in view of the attitude of this country with regard to the effect of the naturalization of foreigners.

This article obligates Germany to recognize any new nationality acquired by her nationals under the laws of the Allied and Associated Powers, and to regard such persons as having, in consequence of the acquisition of such new nationality, in all respects severed their allegiance to their country of origin. The language of the article is carefully framed so as to eliminate any question of dual nationality on the part of a person who casts off his German allegiance. Although the obligations of these provisions are binding on Germany only, it seems possible that the article may have value as a precedent in dealing with the question of conflicts of nationality.

In the section just mentioned the Allied and Associated Powers secure to themselves the right to send consular officers to Germany.

Treaties.

It was of course important that an arrangement should be provided for in the Treaty of Peace with regard to the status of treaties of all sorts to which Germany and the Allied and Associated Powers were parties before the war. The subject was very carefully dealt with by Articles 282 to 295 in a way that should leave little room for future complications. All vexatious questions as to the effect of war on treaties are eliminated.

The treaty enumerates a very considerable list of so-called multilateral treaties—that is, international agreements between three or more nations; and it is declared that such agreements alone shall be applied between Germany and those of the Allied and Associated Powers who are parties thereto.

The subject of bilateral treaties which Germany had concluded with each of the Allied and Associated Powers is dealt with in a different way. These agreements are in effect declared abrogated in the Treaty of Peace. The right is accorded to each of the Allied or Associated Powers to revive, by giving notice to Germany within six months, any treaty or convention which each of the Allied and Associated Powers may desire to continue in effect. Treaty stipulations at variance with the Treaty of Peace may not be revived. In cases of difference of opinion on this point it is provided that appeal shall be made to the decision of the League of Nations.

The scheme for the revival of treaties furnishes a useful procedure for readjusting treaty relations with Germany. With regard to numerous treaties such a readjustment is doubtless highly desirable. It was not regarded as unfair to Germany that only the Allied and Associated Powers should have the right to revive treaties. Apparently no injury can result to Germany from this situation. The treaty prevents nations from splitting up in a manner prejudicial to Germany any treaty it is desired to revive. The treaties that may be revived are independent agreements, such as commercial treaties, consular conventions, and extradition treaties. Generally speaking, they stipulate reciprocal rights in behalf of each of the contracting parties. If one kind of a treaty is revived and another is allowed to lapse because, perhaps, it has become obsolete and is no longer responsive to present needs, both of the contracting parties are similarly affected.

Furthermore, treaties of this character generally contain stipulations under which they can be abrogated on a year's notice by either party. Germany will therefore be able to denounce a treaty which she does not desire to have continued in existence after it has been revived by an Allied or Associated Power.

It is my understanding that the arrangement has peculiar advantages for the United States. Our treaty relations with Germany are based almost entirely on old treaties concluded a long time ago with the independent states, which were united to form the German Empire. I am informed that vexatious questions have arisen from time to time as to the legal effect of these treaties with regard to their application between our Government and the Government of the German Empire, with which they were not negotiated.

The provisions in the Peace Treaty under the heading of Commercial Relations, taken as a whole, would adequately protect our Government's interests during a period in which treaty relations with Germany might be directly adjusted between the two Governments on a more satisfactory basis than that existing before the war. The situation resulting from these stipulations which have been discussed may be briefly summarized.

Provision is made in the treaty for equality of treatment in all matters relating to customs duties and shipping charges. By comprehensive stipulations everything needed in the way of a naturalization treaty is provided. Concise provisions deal with rights of American citizens to do business in Germany, and the protection of their property rights generally. The right to send consular officers to Germany is secured.

The section devoted to treaties contains some further miscellaneous provisions of more or less interest which do not affect the general situation outlined above. They relate chiefly to agreements concluded by Germany with the Allies. Germany is required to recognize as abrogated agreements concluded by her with Austria, Hungary, Bulgaria, or Turkey since the first of August, 1914, until the coming into force of the Peace Treaty. She must similarly recognize as abrogated agreements concluded with Russia or with any state or

Government of which the territory previously formed a part of Russia or with Rumania before August 1, 1914, or after that date until the coming into force of the Peace Treaty.[1] She must secure to the Allied and Associated Powers the benefits granted to Austria, Hungary, Bulgaria, or Turkey by agreements concluded before August 1, 1914.

Debts.

By Article 296 and the Annex thereto a scheme is provided for the settlement of debts due by nationals of the enemy countries to each other as well as certain public debts. The purpose of the scheme is mainly to facilitate an adjustment of private commercial transactions in a complete and expeditious manner, without private litigation, and without the difficulties which might arise out of such litigation as a result of the application of diverse rules and principles by the municipal tribunals of the various countries. The plan of settlement is, briefly stated, as follows:

Clearing offices are established for the settlement of debts between each Allied and Associated Government and Germany. Each of the contracting parties establishes a clearing office for the collection and payment of debts. Sums due to the nationals of one of the contracting parties by nationals of the other will be debited to the clearing office of the country of the debtor, and paid to the credi-

[1]This abrogates the Brest-Litovsk and Bucharest treaties.

tor by the clearing office of the country of the creditor.

The contracting parties obligate themselves to guarantee payments of all debts due by their nationals, with certain exceptions. They further agree to forbid payment of such debts by their nationals and to forbid all communication between the interested persons with regard to the settlement of debts otherwise than through clearing offices.

It is optional with an Allied or Associated state as to whether it will be a party to this scheme of settling debts. Unless within one month from the coming into force of the treaty it gives notice that it desires to participate in the clearing office scheme, the provisions in respect thereof will not apply between it and Germany.

The proceeds of property of German nationals which is within Allied and Associated countries, and which is liquidated in accordance with provisions of the treaty relating to the retention and liquidation of property of enemy nationals, may be used by such countries to pay debts owing to their nationals. Such proceeds will be accounted for through the clearing offices.

The merits of this plan can probably be definitely determined only in the light of experience. Much confusion and controversy, both of a private and a public nature, might perhaps result from the efforts of persons to effect private settlement in the future directly or through the tribunals of each nation. On the other hand, the obligation of a nation to guarantee debts of its nationals might prove a difficult and disagreeable one to carry into effect. And action by a Government to prevent private adjustment of debts might result in an unfortunate interference with private transactions.

Probably a controlling consideration with the Government of the United States, should it become a party to the treaty, would be the objection to a scheme which would make necessary the use of private property of enemy nationals for the specific purpose of satisfying debts, or in any way place restriction on the disposition of such property by this government. Provisions of the treaty, to which I shall later refer, were so framed that Congress will have a free hand in disposing of such property, if the clearing-office scheme shall not be adopted.

With respect to the attitude of the United States relative to these stipulations, it seems pertinent to take into consideration that the situation of nationals of the Allied Governments at the outbreak of the war appears somewhat different from that of citizens of the United States when this country became a belligerent.

The Allies were suddenly plunged into war. The Governments of Great Britain and France, in order to avoid most serious financial disasters at the beginning of the war, had found it necessary to guarantee a great many private obligations, such as acceptances by bankers whose principals were in Germany, and to protect the interests of their citizens in various ways. Long prior to the end of the war, these countries had studied in detail a plan under which debts could be adjusted after the war. The United States entered the conflict two and a half years after the outbreak of the war in Europe, and its citizens had then had an opportunity to adjust their business affairs with Germans to war conditions. Contracts made for some time prior to our entrance into the war must seemingly have been entered into with some knowledge of the risks incurred.

The clearing house plan may be desirable and necessary for some of the Allied countries, but it was considered by the American representatives at Paris that it might be undesirable, if not impossible, for the United States. For that reason they took steps to have the adoption of the scheme made optional.

Property, Rights, and Interests.

Articles 297 and 298 and the Annex following them deal with the disposition of the property of enemy nationals found in the territory of each belligerent nation at the outbreak of war.

During the war the principal belligerent countries had generally taken posession of all or some part of private enemy property within their respective dominions, and in some countries sales of some such property had been made. When the United States entered the war, the taking over of private property and businesses had already proceeded far in other countries, and Congress authorized similar measures here. It became necessary to provide in the treaty for the situation created by such acts. By the Trading with the Enemy Act which contained this authorization it was provided that claims of enemies for seized property should be settled after the end of the war as Congress should direct. This was construed by American representatives on the Peace Commission to mean that the policy of our Government in dealing with such property was not to be determined until after the end of the war, when various facts and conditions which could not be known before that time could be definitely ascertained.

Therefore, in the absence of any defined policy by the United States, we thought it our duty to preserve for Congress unimpaired freedom to deal with all questions relating to enemy property. This seemed the more clearly our duty, since we had no means of ascertaining facts, such as those respecting the treatment of American property by Germany, which might have bearing on a final decision. Consequently, we thought it proper to oppose all suggestions which were made requiring a permanent disposition of the property in any way.

Germany is obligated to restore sequestered property belonging to nationals of the Allied and Associated Powers on demand of the owners "if it still exists in specie," and to pay over the proceeds of property that has been sold. She must make compensation for damages inflicted upon property by the application of "exceptional war measures." Such damages are to be determined by a tribunal of three members.

The Allied and Associated Powers "reserve the right to retain and liquidate" the property of German nationals within their territory, and to hold such property "as a pledge" for the payment of certain obligations due to their nationals. These obligations are: Claims of such nationals in respect of damage committed to their property within German territory; debts owing to them by German nationals, and claims growing out of acts committed by the German Government or any German authorities since July 31, 1914, and before an Allied or Associated Power, desiring to make such claims, entered the war.

The last mentioned class of claims would cover any claims the United States might desire to make on account of the sinking of such vessels as the *Lusitania,* the *Frye,* the *Sussex,* and the *Leelanaw,* or on account of other pre-war acts committed by the German authorities in violation of the rights of American citizens.

German property and the net proceeds resulting from its liquidation may further be charged by the Allied and Associated Powers with the payment of claims of their nationals with regard to their property in territory of other enemy Powers, in so far as those claims are otherwise unsatisfied. Justification of this provision, if advantage is taken of it, will have a basis on the theory of joint responsibility resulting from the fact that Germany and her allies acted as a unit in carrying on the war, and showed by their conduct toward private enemy property that they acted on a similar theory as to joint responsibility on the part of the Allied and Associated Powers.

Any property or proceeds of property not used by an Allied or Associated Power for the purposes just mentioned may be retained, and if retained the cash value thereof must be used to pay the reparation demanded of Germany.

Germany undertakes to compensate her nationals for property retained by the Allied and Associated Governments.

The treaty does not contemplate the taking of property of enemy nationals without some form of compensation. The question of taking of property is left to the determination of each of the Allied or Associated Powers in its own discretion, and if in any case the property is taken for purposes permitted by the treaty Germany is required to make compensation.

The treaty provides that the proceeds of property of German nationals "shall be subject to disposal by such Power in accordance with its laws and regulations."

Therefore, if the United States should ratify the treaty, the power of Congress to deal with German-owned property in the United States would be the same as it was prior to the conclusion of the treaty. There is, therefore, no conflict between the treaty and the Trading with the Enemy Act, by Section 12, of which it is provided, as has been pointed out, that the ultimate disposition of seized property shall be determined by Congress after the war.

The treaty authorizes seizure and liquidation of property on a more extensive scale than that contemplated by the Trading with the Enemy Act.

Under the act the Alien Property Custodian has seized only property of persons resident within German territory and territory under German military occupation, and property of persons whom the President has, pursuant to the act, included within the term "enemy." Under the treaty the Allied and Associated Powers reserve the right to retain and liquidate the property of German nationals within their territories, irrespective of the residence of the owners.

The disposition of such property by each of the Allied and Associated Powers obviously raises a grave question. Irrespective of whether under international law a belligerent country has a strict legal right to confiscate property of enemy nationals within its territory, we know that confiscation has been generally severely condemned in modern times. The practice of confiscation has virtually become obsolete, except in the case of reprisals which can be justified by the disregard of private rights.

As heretofore observed, under the treaty the Government of the United States is not committed to any course which might be regarded as confiscatory. Congress may decide that the property shall be used for any or all of the purposes specified in the treaty, and it may provide for the return of all or a part of the property to its German owners.

The principle of the inviolability of private property which a nation finds within its territory on the outbreak of war has always been upheld by the Government of the United States. And our Government has throughout its existence as a nation championed the establishment of a similar immunity for private property at sea. Whether our Government will abandon these principles and resort to the use of the property of enemy nationals which has been sequestered by the Alien Property Custodian during the war can be settled by Congress alone.

In view of the conditions specified in the treaty under which the Allied and Associated Powers reserve the right to retain property of enemy nationals, the retention of such property would not constitute absolute confiscation. The property can be taken to pay just claims against Germany, debts against German nationals, and the general reparation obligations; and the German Government undertakes to pay its nationals for property so used. It was admitted by Germany that she could not meet her obligations without drawing on the property of her nationals abroad. Some of the Allied Powers utilized the foreign investments of their nationals during the war, giving their own Government securities in exchange.[1]

As has been pointed out, it is optional with the Allied and Associated Powers as to whether or not they will use private property for the payment of claims in the manner authorized by the treaty. Perhaps an effort will be made by the United States, should it become a party to the treaty, and by other nations, to effect some settlement of claims

---

[1]See pp. 338, 339, 340, 341, and 342 in the Addenda.

with the German Government, which will render unnecessary the appropriation of all or any private property for such purpose. It seems possible that under the terms of the treaty the assets of Germany are so pledged for other reparation purposes that none would be available for this particular purpose. However, an interpretation might be given the treaty so as to make possible a settlement of claims for which German-owned property is held as a pledge, so that the pledge would not necessarily need to be retained in order that such a settlement might be effected.

Possibly some nations may see fit to draw a distinction between certain classes of property or between certain classes of persons and effect a disposition of property on a basis of such a distinction. There is a large amount of German Government or quasi-German Government property and perhaps some apparently privately owned property fostered by the German Government, that can be used for the purpose of paying claims. This class of property might well be distinguished from strictly private property.

Contracts, Prescriptions, Judgments.

The considerations relating to the adjustment of pre-war contracts were somewhat similar to those respecting the settlement of pre-war debts. For the European countries the war began suddenly and unexpectedly, abruptly terminating all business relations with Germany. For them the war had lasted more than four years, and the possible injustice of canceling some pre-war contracts that might have survived was considered a negligible factor in view of the great advantage of constituting a definite legal status for all such pending matters. In this situation they concluded that in the interest of all concerned all pre-war contracts should be annulled. On the other hand, in the United States the situation had adjusted itself to a great extent to war conditions in the two and a half years during which the war had lasted before we entered it. Undoubtedly many contracts of an innocent character made before our entrance into the war were still in existence.

Under our jurisprudence the state of war serves to dissolve some classes of contracts and only to suspend others, and our judicial decisions have ruled that those contracts in which no public interest is involved, and the performance of which was not rendered inequitable on account of new conditions produced by the war, it would be unjust and inequitable to disturb. Consequently, the Americans were of opinion that to require the general cancellation of all existing contracts, including those which our courts had decided should not be disturbed, would constitute an unnecessary and unjustifiable interference with the private rights of our citizens, and furthermore might entail substantial claims against our Government.[1]

---

[1]Our views on that subject were expressed in a contemporaneous memorandum that will be found in the Addenda, page 343.

Articles 299 to 303, inclusive, and an Annex following them, deal with contracts entered into with German nationals prior to the war by nationals of the Allied and Associated countries. The general purpose of these provisions is, as in the case of provisions with regard to debts, to prescribe certain definite rules, so that questions concerning such matters as are not governed by international law may not be left altogether to the probable conflicting decisions of national tribunals in the respective countries.

Provision is made for a general dissolution of contracts from the time that the parties to a contract became enemies. Exception to such dissolution is made as to debts or other pecuniary obligations arising out of any act done or money paid under a contract, and further as to particular classes of contracts specified in the treaty.

A general exception to the cancellation of contracts is provided for in the case of any contract of which the execution "shall be required in the general interest," within six months from the date of the coming into force of the treaty, by Allied and Associated Governments of which one of the parties is a national.

If the execution of the contract thus kept alive would, owing to the alteration of trade conditions, cause one of the parties substantial injury, a mixed arbitral tribunal will be empowered to grant the prejudiced party equitable compensation.

As in the case of the provisions relating to debts,

it will be difficult to determine, except in the light of experience, the advantages or disadvantages of these stipulations respecting the dissolution of contracts. The United States, Brazil, and Japan are, by a provision in the treaty, excepted from the greater portion of them. This provision was inserted with a view to avoiding any doubtful questions that might arise from the interference with private rights by treaty stipulations, "having regard to the provisions of the Constitution and law of the United States of America, of Brazil, and of Japan," as stated in Article 299(c). It is to be hoped that American citizens will be largely successful in adjusting their pre-war contractual relations with German nationals directly, or through proper judicial tribunals.

It should be observed that, in case the United States should become a party to the treaty, it will not be entirely excepted from these stipulations respecting contracts. It will not be excluded from Article 301, which prescribed certain rules regarding negotiable instruments; nor from Article 302, which provides that, if a judgment in respect of any dispute which may have arisen has been given during the war by a German court against a national of an Allied or Associated state in a case in which he was not able to make his defense, the Allied or Associated national who has suffered prejudice thereby shall be entitled to recover compensation to be fixed by a mixed arbitral tribunal.

Admittedly some of these provisions relative to the dissolution of contracts are one-sided. An illustration is the provision which confers only on the Allied and Associated Powers the right to maintain in force certain contracts, "in the general interest" (Article 299, b). Another is that which provides a remedy against the decisions of German tribunals rendered during the war, but no such reciprocal remedy against the decisions of courts in the Allied and Associated countries (Article 302). Such provisions will doubtless be found objectionable to persons who hold the view that the treaty should have been framed altogether on the theory that the Allied and Associated Powers should not have permitted themselves to take any steps for the protection of their nationals, the benefits of which should not be accorded also to German nationals. Such persons doubtless fail to take into full account, among other pertinent things, the lack of faith, at the time of the treaty negotiations, on the part of all the Allied and Associated countries in the German Government and the German people.

Mixed Arbitral Tribunal.

By Article 304, a Mixed Arbitral Tribunal is established between each of the Allied and Associated Powers, on the one hand, and Germany, on the other hand. The tribunal is composed of three members, one being appointed by each of the Governments concerned, and the third, who shall act as president, being chosen by agreement between the two Governments, and, failing such agreement, by the Council of the League of Nations or by Mr. Gustave Ador, the former President of Switzerland. The third member must be a national of a country that remained neutral during the war.

This tribunal is given jurisdiction to deal with questions, to which I have called attention, with respect to claims for damages to property of nationals of the Allied and Associated Powers in Germany, debts owing by enemy nationals to each other, and contractual relations between them. Perhaps among the functions of the court claims for damages done to property in Germany is of most interest to American citizens.

Concise rules governing the procedure of the court have been formulated. Certain authority is also conferred upon the court to prescribe such rules. It is provided that the language in which the proceedings are to be conducted shall. unless otherwise agreed, be English, French, Italian, or Japanese, as may be determined by the Allied or Associated Powers concerned. There will probably be no difficulty in any given case in reaching an agreement as to the use of one of the well-known tongues in which the proceedings of similar tribunals are generally conducted. French will doubtless be the language most generally employed by these mixed tribunals. American citizens, if the United States ratifies the treaty, will be enabled to present their cases in English. This should be of considerable convenience to them, and it would entail no hardship on Germany.

A method just and satisfactory to the nations

concerned for the determination of private rights of various kinds seems to have been provided by the establishment of this tribunal.

Industrial Property.

Articles 306-311, inclusive, deal with the readjustment of the rights of the citizens of all of the nations at war, in the matter of industrial, literary, and artistic property—that is, patents, trade-mark registrations, and copyrights.

It is important to bear in mind that these articles deal not only with rights to industrial property as between Germany and the Allied and Associated Powers, but also with rights to industrial property as between the Allied and Associated Powers themselves.

From the very outbreak of hostilities between Germany and the Allies, the filing of applications for letters patent, and for the registration of trade-marks and copyrights in Germany, was greatly hampered by censorship and blockade, and was ultimately prohibited, in so far as the United States was concerned, by a presidential proclamation shortly after the entry of the United States into the war. So also, the payment of Government fees for the maintenance in force of German patents owned by citizens of the United States was inhibited by the proclamation.

Furthermore, inasmuch as the manufacturing facilities of the Allies were being increasingly devoted to the production of materials for carrying on the war, American inventors in other lines could find no field for the exploitation of their invention in any of the belligerent countries, and refrained from filing applications therefor within the periods provided for that purpose in the existing treaties; nor could the American owners of patents in the Allied countries conform to the laws of those countries which, in most cases, required the actual exploitation of the invention on a commercial scale in order to maintain the patent in force. Consequently, American owners of patents granted either by Germany or by the Allied and Associated Powers discovered that, as the result of the war, their patents had, to a large extent, become void, and that their rights of priority for filing valid applications in Germany and in the countries of the Allied and Associated Powers had for the most part lapsed.

This portion of the treaty restores to American citizens the lapsed patents upon the payment of normal fees required for that purpose. It also permits American citizens to file in Germany and in the Allied and Associated countries applications for letters patent with the same claim of priority which they would have possessed if filed within the periods provided for by treaties, conventions, or statutes, relating to the matter. The only restriction upon the rights thus restored is that they shall be subject in the case of patents and designs to the imposition of such conditions as each Allied or Associated Power may deem reasonably necessary for the protection of persons who have manufactured or made use of the invention during the period when the rights had lapsed.

The rights of United States citizens to the continued protection afforded by the patents which they own abroad, and the acquisition of other patents which they were practically prevented from acquiring during the war, is, therefore, taken care of by the treaty; and the rights of third parties, both in this country and abroad, who have had such inventions in use, are properly left to the control of the particular Allied or Associated Powers concerned.

American citizens are particularly concerned with this revival of foreign patents because, as a consequence of the war, foreign patents, in most of the countries, became void for failure to pay the renewal fees, and for failure continuously to exploit the subject matter of the patent. In this regard, the citizens of foreign countries, including Germany, had the absolute advantage that United States patents are granted for an unrestricted term of seventeen years, without any requirement for exploitation of the invention and without renewal fees of any kind. The articles of the treaty providing for the revival of lapsed patents owned by citizens of the United States are, therefore, in the direct interest of the citizens of the United States and to their great advantage.

During the war the Federal Trade Commission, by authority of law, granted licenses to United States citizens under a large number of United States patents owned by German nationals. So also during the war the Alien Property Custodian, by like authority, seized and sold or otherwise liquidated many German-owned patents. Article 306 of the treaty provides that all acts done by virtue of special measures taken during the war under legislative, executive, or administrative authority of any Allied or Associated Power in regard to the rights of German nationals in industrial, literary, or artistic property, shall remain in force and shall continue to maintain their full effect. Consequently, these acts of the Government of the United States, through the Federal Trade Commission and the Alien Property Custodian, are recognized as valid, continuing and unrevoked by the conclusion of peace.

It became necessary during the war for the Allied and Associated Powers to make use of all of the facilities at their command to insure its successful outcome. In so doing, it is quite probable that inventions covered by various German patents were employed. Under peace conditions it would have been necessary for the Government of the United States to pay to the owners of these patents many millions of dollars in the form of royalties, profits, or damages for such infringement. It is, of course, unthinkable that the Government of the United States, or any one acting under its authority, should be called upon to pay tribute to the enemy for things done in the prosecution of the war. Article 306 of the treaty therefore precludes the making of any claim in this regard by Germany or German nationals against the United States or any other of the Allied or Associated Powers (or against any person acting in their behalf or with their assent) for infringement of patents thus used, or for the sale or use of any products incident to the manufacture thereof.

This provision, however, is restricted to acts done by the Government or on its behalf or with its assent. It does not extend to individual infringements of patents having nothing to do with war activities and therefore not concerned with the national defense, and which are, therefore, not in the quasi-contraband class. In so far as the United States is concerned, German-owned patents not already dealt with by the Federal Trade Commission or by the Alien Property Custodian, and which do not come under the category of those used by the Government of the United States, or on its behalf or with its consent in the prosecution of the war, are outside of the provisions of Article 306. They are subsisting private rights not affected by the provisions of the treaty.

Subject to the provisions of national legislation to the contrary, funds resulting from the application of war measures to German industrial property rights are dealt with in the same way as other sums due to German nationals are directed to be dealt with in other provisions of the treaty to which I have called attention. And, similarly, sums produced by any measures taken by the German Government in respect of the rights of nationals of the Allied and Associated Powers are treated in the same way as other debts due from German nationals. Obviously, industrial property has no special characteristic which should take it out of the treatment accorded to property in general, so that these provisions may be regarded as merely confirmatory of the provisions to the same effect in other parts of the treaty relating to property in general.

By a provision of some exceptional interest, the Allied and Associated Powers reserve the right to impose such restriction on industrial, literary, and artistic property, of German nationals "as may be considered necessary for national defense or in the public interest, or for assuring the fair treatment by Germany of the rights of industrial, literary, and artistic property held in German territory by its nationals, or for securing the due fulfillment of all the obligations undertaken by Germany in the present treaty."

In the course of the war it was learned that, in the past, improper use had been made by Germans of their patents in foreign countries, by combinations intended to suppress or hamper the development of foreign industries. The provision above referred to reserves to each of the Allied or Associated Powers the right to impose, after the conclusion of peace, conditions or restrictions on the employment of German-owned industrial property in the several Allied or Associated countries, in cases where the national defense or the public interest may so require. The municipal law of Germany has always had such a reservation, but it is lacking in the legislation of the United States.

In so far as the United States is concerned, therefore, it is important that the treaty makes this reservation, and that it is accepted by Germany, so that in case any improper use by Germans of the American patent system should again take place, the power to deal with it would have been reserved by agreement, and could be put into effect by an act of Congress. Inasmuch as Germany has always had a similar reservation, the effect of this part of the treaty is to place the two countries on practically the same footing. There is no reason to infer from this part of the treaty a purpose on the part of the Allied and Associated Powers to deal with German rights other than in a spirit of justice, and it is unthinkable that these rights should be otherwise dealt with by the Government of the United States.

Articles 309 and 310 of the treaty were not consented to by the United States, and it is particularly stipulated in those articles that they shall not apply as between the United States on the one hand, and Germany on the other.

Article 309 provides that no action shall be brought and no claim made by persons residing or carrying on business within the territory of Germany on the one part, and within the territory of the Allied and Associated Powers on the other, or by persons who are citizens of such powers respectively, or by any one deriving title during the war from such persons, by reason of any action which has taken place within the territory of the other party between the declaration of war and the coming into effect of the treaty, which might constitute an infringement of the rights of industrial, literary, and artistic property, either existing at any time during the war or revived thereafter.

In other words, Article 309 includes a reciprocal release as between Germany on the one hand, and the Allied and Associated Powers on the other hand, of causes of action growing out of the infringement of patents, and other forms of industrial, literary, and artistic property during the war. It was deemed advisable on both ethical and legal grounds to except the United States from this article. The acceptance of the article would have amounted to an agreement by the United States that no suits should be brought for infringement of American-owned German patents in exchange for a similar agreement by Germany that no suits should be brought for infringement of German-owned American patents, for the period covering the war.

It seemed arbitrary for the United States to barter the rights of its citizens to sue in Germany for infringement committed on German soil during the war, in exchange for the right of German citizens to sue for infringement committed on United States soil during the war. We were unable to see why the right of an American citizen to sue in Germany for infringement of his German patent on a typewriting machine, for instance, should be exchanged for the right of a German citizen to sue for infringement of his United States patent on a process for refining oil. Moreover, it is doubtful whether the treaty power of the United States is of so broad a scope as to permit of a sacrifice of the property rights of its own nationals without providing compensation.

Article 310 (from which, as above noted, the United States is excepted) proposes in substance that all license contracts for the exploitation of industrial property and for the reproduction of literary and artistic works entered into before the declaration of war between German subjects on the one part, and the nationals of the Allied and Associated Powers on the other, are to be considered as canceled by the war; with a further provision that the beneficiary of the license shall be entitled to a period of six months in which he may exact from the patentee a new license under conditions which, in default of agreement between the parties, are to be fixed by a special tribunal established for that purpose by the Government of the country in which the patent or the like had been granted.

It may well be doubted whether the outbreak of the war of itself terminated license contracts. If not terminated, the license privileges possessed by citizens of the United States under German-owned United States patents are no doubt valuable to the licensees, and we were unable to find any good reason for their annulment, even if it were within the treaty-making power of the United States. Moreover, it seemed to us more than doubtful whether the provision in Article 310 for the compulsory renewal of such licenses, upon new terms to be exacted from the licensor, would be acceptable to public sentiment in the United States.

I have given a brief and rough outline of provisions originally framed by the so-called Economic Commission for insertion into the treaty. These provisions deal with political questions, commercial and industrial subjects from the standpoint of international relations, and private rights in various aspects. They involve technical and difficult questions of domestic law, of international law, and of international practices. To harmonize views, policies, interests, and legal problems was no simple task. On the one hand, it may appear to some that certain subjects were improperly incorporated into a treaty of peace, or were dealt with too much in detail. On the other hand, it would seem that there should not be too ready criticism of the purpose of the framers of the treaty in seeking by comprehensive stipulations to avoid as far as possible future international or private complications resulting from the interruption by war of intercourse between the Powers and between their respective nationals.

The statement is often heard that the Americans did not protect their national interests in the peace negotiations. This statement, I contend, is at variance with the facts. As regards reparation and economic provisions of the treaty in which, as has been seen, the United States has such an extensive, direct interest, it may be affirmed that no justification for such a statement can be found in the light of even the most critical and technical examination.

REPARATION CLAUSES

Summary of Contents.

REPARATION.

Comment.

SECTION I.

GENERAL PROVISIONS.

ARTICLE 231.

Germany's responsibility.

The Allied and Associated Governments affirm and Germany accepts the responsibility of Germany and her allies for causing all the loss and damage to which the Allied and Associated Governments and their nationals have been subjected as a consequence of the war imposed upon them by the aggression of Germany and her allies.

A moral responsibility for all the consequences of the war, not a financial responsibility.

ARTICLE 232.

Germany's inability to make complete reparation.

The Allied and Associated Governments recognize that the resources of Germany are not adequate, after taking into account permanent diminutions of such resources which will result from other provisions of the present Treaty, to make complete reparation for all such loss and damage

Germany's reparation obligations.

The Allied and Associated Governments, however, require, and Germany undertakes,

This follows substantially the language

that she will make compensation for all damage done to the civilian population of the Allied and Associated Powers and to their property during the period of the belligerency of each as an Allied or Associated Power against Germany by such aggression by land, by sea and from the air, and in general all damage as defined in Annex I hereto.

of the pre-armistice declaration of November 4, 1918, which was accepted by Germany.

Reimbursement to Belgium for her war costs.

In accordance with Germany's pledges, already given, as to complete restoration for Belgium, Germany undertakes, in addition to the compensation for damage elsewhere in this Part provided for, as a consequence of the violation of the Treaty of 1839, to make reimbursements of all sums which Belgium has borrowed from the Allied and Associated Governments up to November 11, 1918, together with interest at the rate of five per cent. (5%) per annum on such sums. This amount shall be determined by the Reparation Commission, and the German Government undertakes thereupon forthwith to make a special issue of bearer bonds to an equivalent amount payable in marks gold, on May 1, 1926, or, at the option of the German Government, on the 1st of May in any year up to 1926. Subject to the foregoing, the form of such bonds shall be determined by the Reparation Commission. Such bonds shall be handed over to the Reparation Commission,

This special position for Belgium is derived from Germany's own admissions as to her liability on account of the violation of Belgian neutrality.

which has authority to take and acknowledge receipt thereof on behalf of Belgium.

ARTICLE 233.

The Reparation Commission, its powers and duties.

The amount of the above damage for which compensation is to be made by Germany shall be determined by an Inter-Allied Commission, to be called the *Reparation Commission* and constituted in the form and with the powers set forth hereunder and in Annexes II to VII inclusive hereto.

This Commission shall consider the claims and give to the German Government a just opportunity to be heard.

The findings of the Commission as to the amount of damage defined as above shall be concluded and notified to the German Government on or before May 1, 1921, as representing the extent of that Government's obligations.

The Commission shall concurrently draw up a schedule of payments prescribing the time and manner for securing and discharging the entire obligation within a period of thirty years from May 1, 1921. If, however, within the period mentioned Germany fails to discharge her obligations, any balance remaining unpaid may within the discretion of the Commission, be postponed for settlement in subsequent years, or may be handled otherwise in such manner as the Allied and Associated Governments, acting in accordance with the procedure laid down in this Part of the present Treaty, shall determine.

The latter part of Art. 233 and Art. 234 makes provision for readjustments and cancellations in the event that the original estimates of Germany's capacity prove erroneous.

Article 234.

The Reparation Commission shall after May 1, 1921, from time to time, consider the resources and capacity of Germany, and, after giving her representatives a just opportunity to be heard, shall have discretion to extend the date, and to modify the form of payments, such as are to be provided for in accordance with Article 233; but not to cancel any part, except with the specific authority of the several Governments represented upon the Commission.

Article 235.

Germany's initial payment.

In order to enable the Allied and Associated Powers to proceed at once to the restoration of their industrial and economic life, pending the full determination of their claims, Germany shall pay in such instalments and in such manner (whether in gold, commodities, ships, securities or otherwise) as the Reparation Commission may fix, during 1919, 1920 and the first four months of 1921, the equivalent of 20,000,000,000 gold marks. Out of this sum the expenses of the armies of occupation subsequent to the Armistice of November 11, 1918, shall first be met, and such supplies of food and raw materials as may be judged by the Governments of the Principal Allied and Associated Powers to be essential to enable Germany to meet her obligations for reparation may also, with the approval of the said Governments, be paid for out of the above sum. The balance shall be reckoned towards liquidation of the amounts due for reparation. Germany shall further deposit bonds as prescribed in paragraph 12 (c) of Annex II hereto.

Provision is made to prevent Germany's initial payment being at the expense of essential food and raw material imports.

Article 236.

Reparation in kind.

Germany further agrees to the direct application of her economic resources to reparation as specified in Annexes III, IV, V, and VI, relating respectively to merchant shipping, to physical restoration, to coal and derivatives of coal, and to dyestuffs and other chemical products; provided always that the value of the property transferred and any services rendered by her under these Annexes, assessed in the manner therein prescribed, shall be credited to her towards liquidation of her obligations under the above Articles.

These deliveries in kind are a credit against the initial and subsequent payments provided for above.

Article 237.

Division of reparation among the damaged nations.

The successive instalments, including the above sum, paid over by Germany in satisfaction of the above claims will be divided by the Allied and Associated Governments in proportions which have been determined upon by them in advance on a basis of general equity and of the rights of each.

For the purposes of this division the value of property transferred and services rendered under Article 243, and under Annexes III, IV, V, VI, and VII, shall be reckoned in the same manner as cash payments effected in that year.

This operates so that nations receiving reparation in kind must account therefor into the General Reparation Fund.

Article 238.

Restitution of stolen articles.

In addition to the payments mentioned above Germany shall effect, in accordance with the procedure laid down by the Reparation Commission, restitution in cash of cash taken away, seized or sequestrated, and also restitution of animals, objects of every nature and securities taken away, seized or sequestrated, in the cases in which it proves possible to identify them in territory belonging to Germany or her allies.

Until this procedure is laid down, restitution will continue in accordance with the provisions of the Armistice of November 11, 1918, and its renewals and the Protocols thereto.

ARTICLE 239.

The German Government undertakes to make forthwith the restitution contemplated by Article 238 and to make the payments and deliveries contemplated by Articles 233, 234, 235 and 236.

ARTICLE 240.

Facilities to be accorded the Reparation Commission.

The German Government recognizes the Commission provided for by Article 233 as the same may be constituted by the Allied and Associated Governments in accordance with Annex II, and agrees irrevocably to the possession and exercise by such Commission of the power and authority given to it under the present Treaty.

The German Government will supply to the Commission all the information which the Commission may require relative to the financial situation and operations and to the property, productive capacity, and stock and current production of raw materials and manufactured articles of Germany and her nationals, and further any information relative to military operations which in the judgment of the Commission may be necessary for the assessment of Germany's liability for reparation as defined in Annex I.

The German Government will accord to the members of the Commission and its authorised agents the same rights and immunities as are enjoyed in Germany by duly accredited diplomatic agents of friendly Powers.

Germany further agrees to provide for the salaries and expenses of the Commission and of such staff as it may employ.

ARTICLE 241.

Germany undertakes to pass, issue and maintain in force any legislation, orders and decrees that may be necessary to give complete effect to these provisions.

ARTICLE 242.

The provisions of this Part of the present Treaty do not apply to the property, rights and interests referred to in Sections III and IV of Part X (Economic Clauses) of the present Treaty, nor to the product of their liquidation, except so far as concerns any final balance in favour of Germany under Article 243 (a).

ARTICLE 243.

Credits in Germany's favor.

The following shall be reckoned as credits to Germany in respect of her reparation obligations:

This provision for credits and particularly Subdivision (c) may operate very materially to relieve the burden of the reparation obligation.

(a) Any final balance in favour of Germany under Section V (Alsace-Lorraine) of Part III (Political Clauses for Europe) and Sections III and IV of Part X (Economic Clauses) of the present Treaty;

(b) Amounts due to Germany in respect of transfers under Section IV (Saar Basin) of Part III (Political Clauses for Europe), Part IX (Financial Clauses), and Part XII (Ports, Waterways and Railways);

(c) Amounts which in the judgment of the Reparation Commission should be credited to Germany on account of any other transfers under the present Treaty of property, rights, concessions or other interests.

In no case however shall credit be given for property restored in accordance with Article 238 of the present Part.

ARTICLE 244.

Cession of cables.

The transfer of the German submarine cables which do not form the subject of particular provisions of the present Treaty is regulated by Annex VII hereto.

ANNEX I.

The categories of damage for which Germany is liable.

This constitutes the agreed interpretation of the pre-armistice declaration. (See Article 232).

Compensation may be claimed from Germany under Article 232 above in respect of the total damage under the following categories:

(1) Damage to injured persons and to surviving dependents by personal injury to

or death of civilians caused by acts of war, including bombardments or other attacks on land, on sea, or from the air, and all the direct consequences thereof, and of all operations of war by the two groups of belligerents wherever arising.

(2) Damage caused by Germany or her allies to civilian victims of acts of cruelty, violence or maltreatment (including injuries to life or health as a consequence of imprisonment, deportation, internment or evacuation, of exposure at sea or of being forced to labour), wherever arising, and to the surviving dependents of such victims.

(3) Damage caused by Germany or her allies in their own territory or in occupied or invaded territory to civilian victims of all acts injurious to health or capacity to work, or to honour, as well as to the surviving dependents of such victims.

(4) Damage caused by any kind of maltreatment of prisoners of war.

(5) As damage caused to the people of the Allied and Associated Powers, all pensions and compensation in the nature of pensions to naval and military victims of war (including members of the air force), whether mutilated, wounded, sick or invalided, and to the dependents of such victims, the amount due to the Allied and Associated Governments being calculated for

each of them as being the capitalised cost of such pensions and compensation at the date of the coming into force of the present Treaty on the basis of the scales in force in France at such date.

(6) The cost of assistance by the Governments of the Allied and Associated Powers to prisoners of war and to their families and dependents.

(7) Allowances by the Governments of the Allied and Associated Powers to the families and dependents of mobilised persons or persons serving with the forces, the amount due to them for each calendar year in which hostilities occurred being calculated for each Government on the basis of the average scale for such payments in force in France during that year.

(8) Damage caused to civilians by being forced by Germany or her allies to labour without just remuneration.

(9) Damage in respect of all property wherever situated belonging to any of the Allied or Associated States or their nationals, with the exception of naval and military works or materials, which has been carried off, seized, injured or destroyed by the acts of Germany or her allies on land, on sea or from the air, or damage directly in consequence of hostilities or of any operations of war.

(10) Damage in the form of levies, fines and other similar exactions imposed by Germany or her allies upon the civilian population.

ANNEX II.

1.

The Reparation Commission.

The Commission referred to in Article 233 shall be called "The Reparation Commission" and is hereinafter referred to as "the Commission."

2.

Its membership.

Delegates to this Commission shall be nominated by the United States of America, Great Britain, France, Italy, Japan, Belgium and the Serb-Croat-Slovene State. Each of these Powers will appoint one Delegate and also one Assistant Delegate, who will take his place in case of illness or necessary absence, but at other times will only have the right to be present at proceedings without taking any part therein.

On no occasion shall the Delegates of more than five of the above Powers have the right to take part in the proceedings of the Commission and to record their votes. The Delegates of the United States, Great Britain, France and Italy shall have this right on all occasions. The Delegate of Belgium shall have this right on all occasions other than those referred to below. The Delegate of Japan shall have this right on occasions when questions relating to damage at sea, and questions arising under Article 260 of Part IX (Financial Clauses) in which Japanese interests are concerned, are under consideration. The Delegate of the Serb-Croat-Slovene State shall have this right when questions relating to Austria, Hungary or Bulgaria are under consideration.

Right of withdrawal.

Each Government represented on the Commission shall have the right to withdraw therefrom upon twelve months' notice filed with the Commission and confirmed in the course of the sixth month after the date of the original notice.

3.

Participation of other interested states.

Such of the other Allied and Associated Powers as may be interested shall have the right to appoint a Delegate to be present and act as Assessor only while their respective claims and interests are under examination or discussion, but without the right to vote.

4.

In case of the death, resignation or recall of any Delegate, Assistant Delegate or Assessor, a successor to him shall be nominated as soon as possible.

5.

Its Bureau.

The Commission will have its principal permanent Bureau in Paris and will hold its first meeting in Paris as soon as practicable after the coming into force of the present Treaty, and thereafter will meet in such place or places and at such time as it may deem convenient and as may be necessary for the most expeditious discharge of its duties.

6.

Its presiding officers.

At its first meeting the Commission shall elect, from among the Delegates referred to above, a Chairman and a Vice-Chairman, who shall hold office for one year and shall be eligible for re-election. If a vacancy in the Chairmanship or Vice-Chairmanship should occur during the annual period, the Commission shall proceed to a new election for the remainder of the said period.

7.

Its employees.

The Commission is authorized to appoint all necessary officers, agents and employees who may be required for the execution of its functions, and to fix their remuneration; to constitute committees, whose members need not necessarily be members of the Commission, and to take all executive steps necessary for the purpose of discharging its duties; and to delegate authority and discretion to officers, agents and committees.

8.

All proceedings of the Commission shall be private, unless, on particular occasions, the Commission shall otherwise determine for special reasons.

9.

Germany's right to be heard.

The Commission shall be required, if the German Government so desire, to hear, within a period which it will fix from time to time, evidence and arguments on the part of Germany on any question connected with her capacity to pay.

10.

The Commission shall consider the claims and give to the German Government a just opportunity to be heard, but not to take any part whatever in the decisions of the Commission. The Commission shall afford a similar opportunity to the allies of Germany, when it shall consider that their interests are in question.

11.

Procedure.

The Commission shall not be bound by any particular code or rules of law or by any particular rule of evidence or of procedure, but shall be guided by justice, equity and good faith. Its decisions must follow the same principles and rules in all cases where they are applicable. It will establish rules relating to methods of proof of claims. It may act on any trustworthy modes of computation.

12.

The Commission as agent of the Allied and Associated Powers and its broad authority.

The Commission shall have all the powers conferred upon it, and shall exercise all the functions assigned to it, by the present Treaty.

These provisions and the unusual authority they confer are designed to make the reparation clauses and the Reparation Commission workable and businesslike in character.

The Commission shall in general have wide latitude as to its control and handling of the whole reparation problem as dealt with in this Part of the present Treaty and shall have authority to interpret its provisions. Subject to the provisions of the present Treaty, the Commission is constituted by the several Allied and Associated Governments referred to in paragraphs 2 and 3 above as the exclusive agency of the said Governments respectively for receiving, selling, holding, and distributing the reparation payments to be made by Germany under this Part of the present Treaty. The Commission must comply with the following conditions and provisions:

Instructions to the Commission.

(a) Whatever part of the full amount of the proved claims is not paid in gold, or in ships, securities and commodities or otherwise, Germany shall be required, under such conditions as the Commission may determine, to cover by way of guarantee by an equivalent issue of bonds, obligations or otherwise, in order to constitute an acknowledgment of the said part of the debt.

(b) In periodically estimating Germany's capacity to pay, the Commission shall examine the German system of taxation, first, to the end that the sums for reparation which Germany is required to pay shall become a charge upon all her revenues prior to that for the service or discharge of any domestic loan, and secondly, so as to satisfy itself that, in general, the German scheme of taxation is fully as heavy proportionately as that of any of the Powers represented on the Commission.

Bond issues.

These bonds cannot be distributed or negotiated without unanimous consent. (See paragraph 13.)

(c) In order to facilitate and continue the immediate restoration of the economic life of the Allied and Associated countries, the Commission will as provided in Article 235 take from Germany by way of security for and acknowledgment of her debt a first instalment of gold bearer bonds free of all taxes and charges of every description established or to be established by the Government of the German Empire or of the German States, or by any authority subject to them; these bonds will be delivered on account and in three portions, the marks gold being payable in conformity with Article 262 of Part IX (Financial Clauses) of the present Treaty as follows:

(1) To be issued forthwith, 20,000,000,000 marks gold bearer bonds, payable not later than May 1, 1921, without interest. There shall be specially applied towards the amortisation of these bonds the payments which Germany is pledged to make in conformity with Article 235, after deduction of the sums used for the reimbursement of expenses of the armies of occupation and for payment of foodstuffs and raw materials. Such bonds as have not been redeemed by May 1, 1921, shall then be exchanged or new bonds of the same type as those provided for below (paragraph 12, c, (2)).

(2) To be issued forthwith, further 40,000,000,000 marks gold bearer bonds, bearing interest at 2½ per cent. per annum between 1921 and 1926, and thereafter at 5 per cent. per annum with an additional 1 per cent. for amortisation beginning in 1926 on the whole amount of the issue.

(3) To be delivered forthwith a covering undertaking in writing to issue when, but not until, the Commission is satisfied that Germany can meet such interest and sinking fund obligations, a further instalment of 40,000,000,000 marks gold 5 per cent.

bearer bonds, the time and mode of payment of principal and interest to be determined by the Commission.

The dates for payment of interest, the manner of applying the amortisation fund, and all other questions relating to the issue, management and regulation of the bond issue shall be determined by the Commission from time to time.

Further issues by way of acknowledgment and security may be required as the Commission subsequently determines from time to time.

(d) In the event of bonds, obligations or other evidence of indebtedness issued by Germany by way of security for or acknowledgment of her reparation debt being disposed of outright, not by way of pledge, to persons other than the several Governments in whose favour Germany's original reparation indebtedness was created, an amount of such reparation indebtedness shall be deemed to be extinguished corresponding to the nominal value of the bonds, etc., so disposed of outright, and the obligation of Germany in respect of such bonds shall be confined to her liabilities to the holders of the bonds, as expressed upon their face.

Evaluation of damages to the invaded areas.

The principle of "replacement value" is here adopted.

(e) The damage for repairing, reconstructing and rebuilding property in the invaded and devastated districts, including reinstallation of furniture, machinery and other equipment, will be calculated according to the cost at the dates when the work is done.

(f) Decisions of the Commission relating to the total or partial cancellation of the capital or interest of any verified debt of Germany must be accompanied by a statement of its reasons.

13.

Voting.

As to voting, the Commission will observe the following rules:

When a decision of the Commission is taken, the votes of all the Delegates entitled to vote, or in the absence of any of them, of their Assistant Delegates, shall be recorded. Abstention from voting is to be treated as a vote against the proposal under discussion. Assessors have no vote.

Matters requiring a unanimous vote.

On the following questions unanimity is necessary:

(a) Questions involving the sovereignty of any of the Allied and Associated Powers, or the cancellation of the whole or any part of the debt or obligations of Germany;

(b) Questions of determining the amount and conditions of bonds or other obligations to be issued by the German Government and of fixing the time and manner for selling, negotiating or distributing such bonds;

(c) Any postponement, total or partial, beyond the end of 1930, of the payment of instalments falling due between May 1, 1921, and the end of 1926 inclusive;

(d) Any postponement, total or partial, of any instalment falling due after 1926 for a period exceeding three years;

(e) Questions of applying in any particular case a method of measuring damages different from that which has been previously applied in a similar case;

(f) Questions of the interpretation of the provisions of this Part of the present Treaty.

All other questions shall be decided by the vote of a majority.

Arbitration of certain differences within the Commission.

In case of any difference of opinion among the Delegates, which cannot be solved by reference to their Governments, upon the question whether a given case is one which requires a unanimous vote for its decision or not, such difference shall be referred to the immediate arbitration of some impartial person to be agreed upon by their Governments, whose award the Allied and Associated Governments agree to accept.

14.

Decisions of the Commission, in accordance with the powers conferred upon it,

The effect of this clause is to render

shall forthwith become binding and may be put into immediate execution without further proceedings.

unnecessary submission of decisions to the Governments represented.

15.

Issue of Participation Certificates to interested Governments.

The Commission will issue to each of the interested Powers, in such form as the Commission shall fix:

(1) A certificate stating that it holds for the account of the said Power bonds of the issues mentioned above, the said certificate, on the demand of the Power concerned, being divisible in a number of parts not exceeding five;

The number of certificates is restricted to avoid a possible tendency of Governments to negotiate the Commission's own certificates.

(2) From time to time certificates stating the goods delivered by Germany on account of her reparation debt which it holds for the account of the said Power.

The said certificates shall be registered, and upon notice to the Commission, may be transferred by endorsement.

When bonds are issued for sale or negotiation, and when goods are delivered by the Commission, certificates to an equivalent value must be withdrawn.

16.

Interest on the Debt.

Interest shall be debited to Germany as from May 1, 1921, in respect of her debt as determined by the Commission, after allowing for sums already covered by cash payments or their equivalent, or by bonds issued to the Commission, or under Article 243. The rate of interest shall be 5 per cent. unless the Commission shall determine at some future time that circumstances justify a variation of this rate.

The Commission, in fixing on May 1, 1921, the total amount of the debt of Germany, may take account of interest due on sums arising out of the reparation of material damage as from November 11, 1918, up to May 1, 1921.

17.

Notification by Commission in case of default.

In case of default by Germany in the performance of any obligation under this Part of the present Treaty, the Commission will forthwith give notice of such default to each of the interested Powers and may make such recommendations as to the action to be taken in consequence of such default as it may think necessary.

18.

Remedies in event of voluntary default.

It is particularly to be noted that these reprisals can be taken only in the event of a *voluntary* default by Germany.

The measures which the Allied and Associated Powers shall have the right to take, in case of voluntary default by Germany, and which Germany agrees not to regard as acts of war, may include economic and financial prohibitions and reprisals and in general such other measures as the respective Governments may determine to be necessary in the circumstances.

19.

Payment may be accepted otherwise than in money or bonds.

Payments required to be made in gold or its equivalent on account of the proved claims of the Allied and Associated Powers may at any time be accepted by the Commission in the form of chattels, properties, commodities, business, rights, concessions, within or without German territory, ships, bonds, shares or securities of any kind, or currencies of Germany or other States, the value of such substitutes for gold being fixed at a fair and just amount by the Commission itself.

This meets a suggestion made by Germany in her observations on the conditions of peace. It is optional with Germany to tender payment in this form under this paragraph.

20.

Rights of Allies and Neutrals to be safeguarded.

The Commission, in fixing or accepting payment in specified properties or rights, shall have due regard for any legal or equitable interests of the Allied and Associated Powers or of neutral Powers or of their nationals therein.

This prevents reparation payments being made at the expense of Allies or Neutrals and out of what is really their property.

21.

No member of the Commission shall be responsible, except to the Government appointing him, for any action or omission as such member. No one of the Allied or Associated Governments assumes any responsibility in respect of any other Government.

22.

Subject to the provisions of the present Treaty this Annex may be amended by the unanimous decision of the Governments represented from time to time upon the Commission.

23.

Dissolution of the Commission.

When all the amounts due from Germany and her allies under the present Treaty or the decisions of the Commission have been discharged and all sums received, or their equivalents, shall have been distributed to the Powers interested, the Commission shall be dissolved.

ANNEX III.

1.

Reparation in kind for shipping losses.

Germany recognises the right of the Allied and Associated Powers to the replacement, ton for ton (gross tonnage) and class for class, of all merchant ships and fishing boats lost or damaged owing to the war.

Nevertheless, and in spite of the fact that the tonnage of German shipping at present in existence is much less than that lost by the Allied and Associated Powers in consequence of the German aggression, the right thus recognised will be enforced on

German ships and boats under the following conditions:

Ships ceded by Germany.

The German Government, on behalf of themselves and so as to bind all other persons interested, cede to the Allied and Associated Governments the property in all the German merchant ships which are of 1,600 tons gross and upwards; in one-half, reckoned in tonnage, of the ships which are between 1,000 tons and 1,600 tons gross; in one-quarter, reckoned in tonnage, of the steam trawlers; and in one-quarter, reckoned in tonnage, of the other fishing boats.

2.

The German Government will, within two months of the coming into force of the present Treaty, deliver to the Reparation Commission all the ships and boats mentioned in paragraph 1.

3.

The ships and boats mentioned in paragraph 1 include all ships and boats which (a) fly, or may be entitled to fly, the German merchant flag; or (b) are owned by any German national, company or corporation or by any company or corporation belonging to a country other than an Allied or Associated country and under the control or direction of German nationals; or (c) are now under construction (1) in Germany, (2) in other than Allied or Associated countries for the account of any German national, company or corporation.

4.

Documents of title.

For the purpose of providing documents of title for the ships and boats to be handed over as above mentioned, the German Government will:

(a) Deliver to the Reparation Commission in respect of each vessel a bill of sale or other document of title evidencing the transfer to the Commission of the entire property in the vessel, free from all encumbrances, charges and liens of all kinds, as the Commission may require;

(b) Take all measures that may be indicated by the Reparation Commission for ensuring that the ships themselves shall be placed at its disposal.

5.

Ships to be built for Allied account.

As an additional part of reparation, Germany agrees to cause merchant ships to be built in German yards for the account of Allied and Associated Governments as follows:

(a) Within three months of the coming into force of the present Treaty, the Reparation Commission will notify to the German

Government the amount of tonnage to be laid down in German shipyards in each of the two years next succeeding the three months mentioned above.

(b) Within two years of the coming into force of the present Treaty, the Reparation Commission will notify to the German Government the amount of tonnage to be laid down in each of the three years following the two years mentioned above.

(c) The amount of tonnage to be laid down in each year shall not exceed 200,000 tons, gross tonnage.

(d) The specifications of the ships to be built, the conditions under which they are to be built and delivered, the price per ton at which they are to be accounted for by the Reparation Commission, and all other questions relating to the accounting, ordering, building and delivery of the ships, shall be determined by the Commission.

6.

Germany undertakes to restore in kind and in normal condition of upkeep to the Allied and Associated Powers, within two months of the coming into force of the present Treaty, in accordance with procedure to be laid down by the Reparation Commission, any boats and other movable appliances belonging to inland navigation which since August 1, 1914, have by any means whatever come into her possession or into the possession of her nationals, and which can be identified.

With a view to make good the loss in inland navigation tonnage, from whatever cause arising, which has been incurred during the war by the Allied and Associated Powers, and which cannot be made good by means of the restitution prescribed above, Germany agrees to cede to the Reparation Commission a portion of the German river fleet up to the amount of the loss mentioned above, provided that such cession shall not exceed 20 per cent. of the river fleet as it existed on November 11, 1918.

The conditions of this cession shall be settled by the arbitrators referred to in Article 339 of Part XII (Ports, Waterways and Railways) of the present Treaty, who are charged with the settlement of difficulties relating to the apportionment of river tonnage resulting from the new international régime applicable to certain river systems or from the territorial changes affecting those systems.

7.

Germany agrees to take any measures that may be indicated to her by the Reparation Commission for obtaining the full title to the property in all ships which have during the war been transferred, or are in process of transfer, to neutral flags, without the consent of the Allied and Associated Governments.

8.

Waiver of shipping claims by Germany.

Germany waives all claims of any description against the Allied and Associated Governments and their nationals in respect of the detention, employment, loss or damage of any German ships or boats, exception being made of payments due in respect of the employment of ships in conformity with the Armistice Agreement of January 13, 1919, and subsequent Agreements.

This exception is so that Germany will receive compensation for ships leased by her to the Allies during the armistice for relief and repatriation purposes.

The handing over of the ships of the German mercantile marine must be continued without interruption in accordance with the said Agreement.

9.

Germany waives all claims to vessels or cargoes sunk by or in consequence of naval action and subsequently salved, in which any of the Allied or Associated Governments or their nationals may have any interest either as owners, charterers, insurers or otherwise, notwithstanding any decree of condemnation which may have been made by a Prize Court of Germany or of her allies.

ANNEX IV.

1.

Reparation in kind for the devastated areas.

The Allied and Associated Powers require, and Germany undertakes, that in part satisfaction of her obligations expressed in the present Part she will, as hereinafter provided, devote her economic resources directly to the physical restoration of the invaded areas of the Allied and Associated Powers, to the extent that these Powers may determine.

2.

The Allied and Associated Governments may file with the Reparation Commission lists showing:

Articles to be replaced.

(a) Animals, machinery, equipment, tools and like articles of a commercial character, which have been seized, consumed or destroyed by Germany or destroyed in direct consequence of military operations, and which such Governments for the purpose of meeting immediate and urgent needs, desire to have replaced by animals and articles of the same nature which are in being in German territory at the date of the coming into force of the present Treaty;

(b) Reconstruction materials (stones, bricks, refractory bricks, tiles, wood, window-glass, steel, lime, cement, etc.), machinery, heating apparatus, furniture and like articles of a commercial character which the said Governments desire to have produced and manufactured in Germany and delivered to them to permit of the restoration of the invaded areas.

3.

Lists to be filed with the Commission.

The lists relating to the articles mentioned in 2 (a) above shall be filed within sixty days after the date of the coming into force of the present Treaty.

The lists relating to the articles in 2 (b) above shall be filed on or before December 31, 1919.

The lists shall contain all such details as are customary in commercial contracts dealing with the subject matter, including specifications, dates of delivery (but not extending over more than four years), and places of delivery, but not price or value, which shall be fixed as hereinafter provided by the Commission.

4.

Action on lists by the Commission.

The Commission is bound to take into account the maintenance of Germany's economic life and to give Germany an opportunity to be heard.

Immediately upon the filing of such lists with the Commission, the Commission shall consider the amount and number of the materials and animals mentioned in the lists provided for above which are to be required of Germany. In reaching a decision on this matter the Commission shall take into account such domestic requirements of Germany as it deems essential for the maintenance of Germany's social and economic life, the prices and dates at which similar articles can be obtained in the Allied and Associated countries as compared with those to be fixed for German articles, and the general interest of the Allied and Associated Governments that the industrial life of Germany be not so disorganised as to affect adversely the ability of Germany to perform the other acts of reparation stipulated for.

Machinery, equipment, tools and like articles of a commercial character in actual industrial use are not, however, to be demanded of Germany unless there is no free stock of such articles respectively which is not in use and is available, and then not in excess of 30 per cent. of the quantity of such articles in use in any one establishment or undertaking.

The Commission shall give representatives of the German Government an opportunity and a time to be heard as to their capacity to furnish the said materials, articles and animals.

The decision of the Commission shall thereupon and at the earliest possible moment be communicated to the German Government and to the several interested Allied and Associated Governments.

The German Government undertakes to deliver the materials, articles and animals as specified in the said communication, and the interested Allied and Associated Governments severally agree to accept the same, provided they conform to the specification given, or are not, in the judgment of the Commission, unfit to be utilized in the work of reparation.

5.

Valuation of articles delivered.

The Commission shall determine the value to be attributed to the materials, articles and animals to be delivered in accordance with the foregoing, and the Allied or Associated Power receiving the same agrees to be charged with such value, and the amount thereof shall be treated as a payment by Germany to be divided in accordance with Article 237 of this Part of the present Treaty.

In cases where the right to require physical restoration as above provided is exercised, the Commission shall ensure that the amount to be credited against the reparation obligation of Germany shall be the fair value of work done or materials supplied by Germany, and that the claim made by the interested Power in respect of the damage so repaired by physical restoration shall be discharged to the extent of the proportion which the damage thus repaired bears to the whole of the damage thus claimed for.

6.

Immediate deliveries of animals.

As an immediate advance on account of the animals referred to in paragraph 2 (a) above, Germany undertakes to deliver in equal monthly instalments in the three months following the coming into force of the present Treaty the following quantities of live stock:

(1) *To the French Government.*

500 stallions (3 to 7 years);
30,000 fillies and mares (18 months to 7 years), type: Ardennais, Boulonnais or Belgian;
2,000 bulls (18 months to 3 years);
90,000 milch cows (2 to 6 years);
1,000 rams;
100,000 sheep;
10.000 goats.

(2) *To the Belgian Government*

200 stallions (3 to 7 years), large Belgian type;
5,000 mares (3 to 7 years), large Belgian type;
5,000 fillies (18 months to 3 years), large Belgian type;

2,000 bulls (18 months to 3 years);
50,000 milch cows (2 to 6 years);
40,000 heifers;
200 rams;
20,000 sheep;
15,000 sows.

The animals delivered shall be of average health and condition.

To the extent that animals so delivered cannot be identified as animals taken away or seized, the value of such animals shall be credited against the reparation obligations of Germany in accordance with paragraph 5 of this Annex.

7.

Without waiting for the decisions of the Commission referred to in paragraph 4 of this Annex to be taken, Germany must continue the delivery to France of the agricultural material referred to in Article III of the renewal dated January 16, 1919, of the Armistice.

ANNEX V.

1

Reparation in the form of coal and coal products.

Germany accords the following options for the delivery of coal and derivatives of coal to the undermentioned signatories of the present Treaty.

2.

For France.

The second provision of the paragraph, providing for the replacement of production of destroyed coal mines, has a priority. (See Paragraph 10.)

Germany undertakes to deliver to France seven million tons of coal per year for ten years. In addition, Germany undertakes to deliver to France annually for a period not exceeding ten years an amount of coal equal to the difference between the annual production before the war of the coal mines of the Nord and Pas de Calais, destroyed as a result of the war, and the production of the mines of the same area during the years in question: such delivery not to exceed twenty million tons in any one year of the first five years, and eight million tons in any one year of the succeeding five years.

It is understood that due diligence will be exercised in the restoration of the destroyed mines in the Nord and the Pas de Calais.

3.

For Belgium.

Germany undertakes to deliver to Belgium eight million tons of coal annually for ten years.

4.

For Italy.

Germany undertakes to deliver to Italy up to the following quantities of coal:

July 1919 to June 1920..	4½ million tons,	
— 1920 — 1921..	6	—
— 1921 — 1922..	7½	—
— 1922 — 1923..	8	—
— 1923 — 1924..	8½	—
and each of the following five years............	8½	—

At least two-thirds of the actual deliveries to be land-borne.

5.

For Luxemburg.

Germany further undertakes to deliver annually to Luxemburg, if directed by the Reparation Commission, a quantity of coal equal to the pre-war annual consumption of German coal in Luxemburg.

6.

Prices for coal.

The prices to be paid for coal delivered under these options shall be as follows:

(a) For overland delivery, including delivery by barge, the German pithead price to German nationals, plus the freight to French, Belgian, Italian or Luxemburg frontiers, provided that the pithead price does not exceed the pithead price of British coal for export. In the case of Belgian bunker coal, the price shall not exceed the Dutch bunker price.

Railroad and barge tariffs shall not be higher than the lowest similar rates paid in Germany.

(b) For sea delivery, the German export price f. o. b. German ports, or the British export price f. o. b. British ports, whichever may be lower.

7.

The Allied and Associated Governments interested may demand the delivery, in place of coal, of metallurgical coke in the proportion of 3 tons of coke to 4 tons of coal.

8.

Coal products.

Germany undertakes to deliver to France, and to transport to the French frontier by rail or by water, the following products, during each of the three years following the coming into force of this Treaty:

Benzol	35,000 tons.
Coal tar..............	50,000 tons.
Sulphate of ammonia..	30,000 tons.

All or part of the coal tar may, at the option of the French Government, be replaced by corresponding quantities of products of distillation, such as light oils, heavy oils, anthracene, naphthalene or pitch.

9.

Coke.

The price paid for coke and for the articles referred to in the preceding paragraph shall be the same as the price paid by German nationals under the same conditions of shipment to the French frontier or to the German ports, and shall be subject to any advantages which may be accorded similar products furnished to German nationals.

10.

Supervision and modification by Reparation Commission.

The Commission is required to take into account the industrial requirements of Germany and may modify the coal deliveries accordingly.

The foregoing options shall be exercised through the intervention of the Reparation Commission, which, subject to the specific provisions hereof, shall have power to determine all questions relative to procedure and the qualities and quantities of products, the quantity of coke which may be substituted for coal, and the times and modes of delivery and payment. In giving notice to the German Government of the foregoing options the Commission shall give at least 120 days' notice of deliveries to be made after January 1, 1920, and at least 30 days' notice of deliveries to be made between the coming into force of this Treaty and January 1, 1920. Until Germany has received the demands referred to in this paragraph, the provisions of the Protocol of December 25, 1918, (Execution of Article VI of the Armistice of November 11, 1918) remain in force. The notice to be given to the German Government of the exercise of the right of substitution accorded by paragraphs 7 and 8 shall be such as the Reparation Commission may consider sufficient. If the

Commission shall determine that the full exercise of the foregoing options would interfere unduly with the industrial requirements of Germany, the Commission is authorised to postpone or to cancel deliveries, and in so doing to settle all questions of priority; but the coal to replace coal from destroyed mines shall receive priority over other deliveries.

ANNEX VI.

1.

Reparation in the form of dyestuff and chemical deliveries.

Germany accords to the Reparation Commission an option to require as part of reparation the delivery by Germany of such quantities and kinds of dyestuffs and chemical drugs as the Commission may designate, not exceeding 50 per cent. of the total stock of each and every kind of dyestuff and chemical drug in Germany or under German control at the date of the coming into force of the present Treaty.

This option shall be exercised within sixty days of the receipt by the Commission of such particulars as to stocks as may be considered necessary by the Commission.

2.

Germany further accords to the Reparation Commission an option to require delivery during the period from the date of the coming into force of the present Treaty until January 1, 1920, and during each period of six months thereafter until January 1, 1925, of any specified kind of dyestuff and chemical drug up to an amount not exceeding 25 per cent. of the German production of such dyestuffs and chemical drugs during the previous six months period. If in any case the production during such previous six months was, in the opinion of the Commission, less than normal, the amount required may be 25 per cent. of the normal production.

Such option shall be exercised within four weeks after the receipt of such particulars as to production and in such form as may be considered necessary by the Commission; these particulars shall be furnished by the German Government immediately after the expiration of each six months period.

3.

For dyestuffs and chemical drugs delivered under paragraph 1, the price shall be fixed by the Commission having regard to pre-war net export prices and to subsequent increases of cost.

For dyestuffs and chemical drugs delivered under paragraph 2, the price shall be fixed by the Commission having regard to pre-war net export prices and subsequent variations of costs, or the lowest net selling price of similar dyestuffs and chemical drugs to any other purchaser.

4.

All details, including mode and times of exercising the options, and making delivery, and all other questions arising under this arrangement shall be determined by the Reparation Commission; the German Government will furnish to the Commission all necessary information and other assistance which it may require.

5.

The above expression "dyestuffs and chemical drugs" includes all synthetic dyes and drugs and intermediate or other products used in connection with dyeing, so far as they are manufactured for sale. The present arrangement shall also apply to cinchona bark and salts of quinine.

ANNEX VII.

Cables ceded.

Germany renounces on her own behalf and on behalf of her nationals in favour of the Principal Allied and Associated Powers all rights, titles or privileges of whatever nature in the submarine cables set out below, or in any portions thereof:

Emden-Vigo: from the Straits of Dover to off Vigo;

Emden-Brest: from off Cherbourg to Brest;

Emden-Teneriffe: from off Dunkirk to off Teneriffe;

Emden-Azores (1): from the Straits of Dover to Fayal;

Emden-Azores (2): from the Straits of Dover to Fayal;

Azores-New-York (1): from Fayal to New York;

Azores-New-York (2): from Fayal to the longitude of Halifax;

Teneriffe-Monrovia: from off Teneriffe to off Monrovia;

Monrovia-Lome:

from about	lat.	:2° 30′ N.;
	long.	:7° 40′ W. of Greenwich;
to about...	lat.	:2° 20′ N.;
	long.	:5° 30′ W. of Greenwich;
and from	lat.	:3° 48′ N.;
about.....	long.	:0° 00′

to Lome;

Lome-Duala: from Lome to Duala;

Monrovia-Pernambuco: from off Monrovia to off Pernambuco;

Constantinople-Constanza: from Constantinople to Constanza;

Yap-Shanghai, Yap-Guam, and Yap-Menado (Celebes): from Yap Island to Shanghai, from Yap Island to Guam Island, and from Yap Island to Menado.

The value of the above mentioned cables or portions thereof in so far as they are privately owned, calculated on the basis of the original cost less a suitable allowance for depreciation, shall be credited to Germany in the reparation account.

SECTION II.

SPECIAL PROVISIONS.

ARTICLE 245.

Special articles to be restored.

Within six months after the coming into force of the present Treaty the German Government must restore to the French Government the trophies, archives, historical souvenirs or works of art carried away from France by the German authorities in the course of the war of 1870-1871 and during this last war, in accordance with a list which will be communicated to it by the French Government; particularly the French flags taken in the course of the war of 1870-1871 and all the political papers taken by the German authorities on October 10, 1870, at the château of Cerçay, near Brunoy (Seine-et-Oise) belonging at the time to Mr. Ruher, formerly Minister of State.

To France.

ARTICLE 246.

To the Hedjaz.

Within six months from the coming into force of the present Treaty, Germany will restore to His Majesty the King of the Hedjaz the original Koran of the Caliph Othman, which was removed from Medina by the Turkish authorities and is stated to have been presented to the ex-Emperor William II.

To Great Britain.

Within the same period Germany will hand over to His Britannic Majesty's Government the skull of the Sultan Mkwawa which was removed from the Protectorate of German East Africa and taken to Germany.

The delivery of the articles above referred to will be effected in such place and in such conditions as may be laid down by the Governments to which they are to be restored.

ARTICLE 247.

To Belgium.

Germany undertakes to furnish to the University of Louvain, within three months after a request made by it and transmitted through the intervention of the Reparation Commission, manuscripts, incunabula, printed books, maps and objects of collection corresponding in number and value to those destroyed in the burning by Germany of the Library of Louvain. All details regarding such replacement will be determined by the Reparation Commission.

Germany undertakes to deliver to Belgium, through the Reparation Commission, within six months of the coming into force of the present Treaty, in order to enable Belgium to reconstitute two great artistic works:

(1) The leaves of the triptych of the Mystic Lamb painted by the Van Eyck brothers, formerly in the Church of St. Bavon at Ghent, now in the Berlin Museum;

(2) The leaves of the triptych of the Last Supper, painted by Dierick Bouts, formerly in the Church of St. Peter at Louvain, two of which are now in the Berlin Museum and two in the Old Pinakothek at Munich.

PART IX.

FINANCIAL CLAUSES.

ARTICLE 248.

Reparation and Treaty costs a first charge on German public assets.

Subject to such exceptions as the Reparation Commission may approve, a first charge upon all the assets and revenues of the German Empire and its constituent States shall be the cost of reparation and all other costs arising under the present Treaty or any treaties or agreements supplementary

The Reparation Commission may create exceptions, and thus provide for Germany raising money for other than Treaty purposes. The charge does not extend thereto or under arrangements concluded between Germany and the Allied and Associated Powers during the Armistice or its extensions.

to the assets of *private* persons, only to *public* property.

Control of export of gold.

Up to May 1, 1921, the German Government shall not export or dispose of, and shall forbid the export or disposal of, gold without the previous approval of the Allied and Associated Powers acting through the Reparation Commission.

ARTICLE 249.

Costs of the armies of occupation.

There shall be paid by the German Government the total cost of all armies of the Allied and Associated Governments in occupied German territory from the date of the signature of the Armistice of November 11, 1918, including the keep of men and beasts, lodging and billeting, pay and allowances, salaries and wages, bedding, heating, lighting, clothing, equipment, harness and saddlery, armament and rolling-stock, air services, treatment of sick and wounded, veterinary and remount services, transport service of all sorts (such as by rail, sea or river, motor lorries), communications and correspondence, and in general the cost of all administrative or technical services the working of which is necessary for the training of troops and for keeping their numbers up to strength and preserving their military efficiency.

The cost of such liabilities under the above heads so far as they relate to purchases or requisitions by the Allied and Associated Governments in the occupied territories shall be paid by the German Government to the Allied and Associated Governments in marks at the current or agreed rate of exchange. All other of the above costs shall be paid in gold marks.

ARTICLE 250.

Germany confirms the surrender of all material handed over to the Allied and Associated Powers in accordance with the Armistice of November 11, 1918, and subsequent Armistice Agreements, and recognises the title of the Allied and Associated Powers to such material.

Non-military property surrendered under the Armistice to be credited to Germany.

There shall be credited to the German Government, against the sums due from it to the Allied and Associated Powers for reparation, the value, as assessed by the Reparation Commission, referred to in Article 233 of Part VIII (Reparation) of the present Treaty, of the material handed over in accordance with Article VII of the Armistice of November 11, 1918, or Article III of the Armistice Agreement of January 16, 1919, as well as of any other material handed over in accordance with the Armistice of November 11, 1918, and of subsequent Armistice Agreements, for which, as having non-military value, credit should in the judgment of the Reparation Commission be allowed to the German Government.

Property belonging to the Allied and Associated Governments or their nationals restored or surrendered under the Armistice Agreements in specie shall not be credited to the German Government.

ARTICLE 251.

Relative priority of Treaty charges.

The priority of the charges established by Article 248 shall, subject to the qualifications made below, be as follows:

(a) The cost of the armies of occupation as defined under Article 249 during the Armistice and its extensions;

(b) The cost of any armies of occupation as defined under Article 249 after the coming into force of the present Treaty;

(c) The cost of reparation arising out of the present Treaty or any treaties or conventions supplementary thereto;

(d) The cost of all other obligations incumbent on Germany under the Armistice Conventions or under this Treaty or any treaties or conventions supplementary thereto.

The payment for such supplies of food and raw material for Germany and such other payments as may be judged by the Allied and Associated Powers to be essential to enable Germany to meet her obligations in respect of reparation will have priority to the extent and upon the conditions which have been or may be determined by the Governments of the said Powers.

This further provision for safeguarding Germany's food and raw material requirements supplements Article 235 which applies only until May 1, 1921.

Article 252.

The right of each of the Allied and Associated Powers to dispose of enemy assets and property within its jurisdiction at the date of the coming into force of the present Treaty is not affected by the foregoing provisions.

Article 253.

Nothing in the foregoing provisions shall prejudice in any manner charges or mortgages lawfully effected in favour of the Allied or Associated Powers or their nationals respectively, before the date at which a state of war existed between Germany and the Allied or Associated Power concerned, by the German Empire or its constituent States, or by German nationals, on assets in their ownership at that date.

ARTICLE 254.

Credit to Germany on account of pre-war debt attributable to ceded territory.

The Powers to which German territory is ceded shall, subject to the qualifications made in Article 255, undertake to pay:

(1) A portion of the debt of the German Empire as it stood on August 1, 1914, calculated on the basis of the ratio between the average for the three financial years 1911, 1912, 1913, of such revenues of the ceded territory, and the average for the same years of such revenues of the whole German Empire as in the judgment of the Reparation Commission are best calculated to represent the relative ability of the respective territories to make payment;

(2) A portion of the debt as it stood on August 1, 1914, of the German State to which the ceded territory belonged, to be determined in accordance with the principle stated above.

Such portions shall be determined by the Reparation Commission.

The method of discharging the obligation, both in respect of capital and of interest, so assumed shall be fixed by the Reparation Commission. Such method may take the form, *inter alia,* of the assumption by the Power to which the territory is ceded of Germany's liability for the German debt held by her nationals. But in the event of the method adopted involving any payments to the German Government, such payments shall be transferred to the Reparation Commission on account of the sums due for reparation so long as any balance in respect of such sums remains unpaid.

ARTICLE 255.

Exception in the case of Alsace-Lorraine.

This exception is based on the like action of Germany in 1871.

(1) As an exception to the above provision and inasmuch as in 1871 Germany refused to undertake any portion of the burden of the French debt, France shall be, in respect of Alsace-Lorraine, exempt from any payment under Article 254.

Partial exception in the case of Poland.

(2) In the case of Poland that portion of the debt which, in the opinion of the Reparation Commission, is attributable to the measures taken by the German and Prussian Governments for the German colonisation of Poland shall be excluded from the apportionment to be made under Article 254.

(3) In the case of all ceded territories other than Alsace-Lorraine, that portion of the debt of the German Empire or German States which, in the opinion of the Repara-

tion Commission, represents expenditure by the Governments of the German Empire or States upon the Government properties referred to in Article 256 shall be excluded from the apportionment to be made under Article 254

ARTICLE 256.

Credit to Germany for public property in ceded territory.

Powers to which German territory is ceded shall acquire all property and possessions situated therein belonging to the German Empire or to the German States, and the value of such acquisitions shall be fixed by the Reparation Commission, and paid by the State acquiring the territory to the Reparation Commission for the credit of the German Government on account of the sums due for reparation.

For the purposes of this Article the property and possessions of the German Empire and States shall be deemed to include all the property of the Crown, the Empire or the States, and the private property of the former German Emperor and other Royal personages.

Exception in the case of Alsace-Lorraine.

This again is based on Germany's like action in 1871.

In view of the terms on which Alsace-Lorraine was ceded to Germany in 1871, France shall be exempt in respect thereof from making any payment or credit under this Article for any property or possessions of the German Empire or States situated therein.

Belgium also shall be exempt from making any payment or any credit under this Article for any property or possessions of the German Empire or States situated in German territory ceded to Belgium under the present Treaty.

ARTICLE 257.

No German debt allocated to territory to be administered under a mandate.

In the case of the former German territories, including colonies, protectorates or dependencies, administered by a Mandatory under Article 22 of Part I (League of Nations) of the present Treaty, neither the territory nor the Mandatory Power shall be charged with any portion of the debt of the German Empire or States.

All property and possessions belonging to the German Empire or to the German States situated in such territories shall be transferred with the territories to the Mandatory Power in its capacity as such and no payment shall be made nor any credit given to those Governments in consideration of this transfer.

For the purposes of this Article the property and possessions of the German Empire and of the German States shall be deemed to include all the property of the Crown, the Empire or the States and the private property of the former German Emperor and other Royal personages.

ARTICLE 258.

Waiver by Germany of special rights in banks, etc., of her former allies and in Russia.

Germany renounces all rights accorded to her or her nationals by treaties, conventions or agreements, of whatsoever kind, to representation upon or participation in the control or administration of commissions, state banks, agencies or other financial or economic organizations of an international character, exercising powers of control or administration, and operating in any of the Allied or Associated States, or in Austria, Hungary, Bulgaria or Turkey, or in the dependencies of these States, or in the former Russian Empire.

ARTICLE 259.

Financial adjustments with respect to Turkey, Austria-Hungary, Roumania and Russia.

(1) Germany agrees to deliver within one month from the date of the coming into force of the present Treaty, to such authority as the Principal Allied and Associated Powers may designate, the sum in gold which was to be deposited in the Reichsbank in the name of the Council of the Administration of the Ottoman Public Debt as security for the first issue of Turkish Government currency notes.

(2) Germany recognises her obligation to make annually for the period of twelve years the payments in gold for which provision is made in the German Treasury Bonds de-

posited by her from time to time in the name of the Council of the Administration of the Ottoman Public Debt as security for the second and subsequent issues of Turkish Government currency notes.

(3) Germany undertakes to deliver, within one month from the coming into force of the present Treaty, to such authority as the Principal Allied and Associated Powers may designate, the gold deposit constituted in the Reichsbank or elsewhere, representing the residue of the advance in gold agreed to on May 5, 1915, by the Council of the Administration of the Ottoman Public Debt to the Imperial Ottoman Government.

(4) Germany agrees to transfer to the Principal Allied and Associated Powers any title that she may have to the sum in gold and silver transmitted by her to the Turkish Ministry of Finance in November, 1918, in anticipation of the payment to be made in May, 1919, for the service of the Turkish Internal Loan.

(5) Germany undertakes to transfer to the Principal Allied and Associated Powers, within a period of one month from the coming into force of the present Treaty, any sums in gold transferred as pledge or as collateral security to the German Government or its nationals in connection with

loans made by them to the Austro-Hungarian Government.

(6) Without prejudice to Article 292 of Part X (Economic Clauses) of the present Treaty, Germany confirms the renunciation provided for in Article XV of the Armistice of November 11, 1918, of any benefit disclosed by the Treaties of Bucharest and of Brest-Litovsk and by the treaties supplementary thereto.

Germany undertakes to transfer, either to Roumania or to the Principal Allied and Associated Powers as the case may be, all monetary instruments, specie, securities and negotiable instruments, or goods, which she has received under the aforesaid Treaties.

(7) The sums of money and all securities, instruments and goods of whatsoever nature, to be delivered, paid and transferred under the provisions of this Article, shall be disposed of by the Principal Allied and Associated Powers in a manner hereafter to be determined by these Powers.

ARTICLE 260.

Agreement by Germany to cede rights in public utilities and concessions in certain States.

Without prejudice to the renunciation of any rights by Germany on behalf of herself or of her nationals in the other provisions of the present Treaty, the Reparation Commission may within one year from the coming into force of the present Treaty demand that the German Government become possessed of any rights and interests of German nationals in any public utility undertaking or in any concession operating in Russia, China, Turkey, Austria, Hungary and Bulgaria, or in the possessions or dependencies of these States or in any territory formerly belonging to Germany or her allies, to be ceded by Germany or her allies to any Power or to be administered by a Mandatory under the present Treaty, and may require that the German Government transfer, within six months of the date of demand, all such rights and interests and any similar rights and interests the German Government may itself possess to the Reparation Commission.

Private owners who are dispossessed to be indemnified by the German Government.

Germany shall be responsible for indemnifying her nationals so dispossessed, and the Reparation Commission shall credit Germany, on account of sums due for reparation, with such sums in respect of the value of the transferred rights and interests as may be assessed by the Reparation Commission, and the German Government shall, within six months from the coming into force of the present Treaty, communicate to the Reparation Commission all such rights and interests, whether already granted, contingent or not yet exercised, and shall renounce on behalf of itself and its nationals in favour of the Allied and Associated Powers all such rights and interests which have not been so communicated.

ARTICLE 261.

German claims against her former allies to be transferred to the Allied and Associated Powers.

Germany undertakes to transfer to the Allied and Associated Powers any claims she may have to payment or repayment by the Governments of Austria, Hungary, Bulgaria or Turkey, and, in particular, any claims which may arise, now or hereafter, from the fulfilment of undertakings made by Germany during the war to those Governments.

ARTICLE 262.

Definition of "gold marks" and optional payment in other currencies.

Any monetary obligation due by Germany arising out of the present Treaty and expressed in terms of gold marks shall be payable at the option of the creditors in pounds sterling payable in London; gold dollars of the United States of America payable in New York; gold francs payable in Paris; or gold lire payable in Rome.

For the purpose of this Article the gold coins mentioned above shall be defined as being of the weight and fineness of gold as enacted by law on January 1, 1914.

ARTICLE 263.

pecial
:paration
Brazil.

Germany gives a guarantee to the Brazilian Government that all sums representing the sale of coffee belonging to the State of Sao Paolo in the ports of Hamburg, Bremen, Antwerp and Trieste, which were deposited with the Bank of Bleichröder at Berlin, shall be reimbursed together with interest at the rate or rates agreed upon. Germany having prevented the transfer of the sums in question to the State of Sao Paolo at the proper time, guarantees also that the reimbursement shall be effected at the rate of exchange of the day of the deposit.

ECONOMIC CLAUSES

Attached to the text of the Economic Clauses as here printed are marginal notes which were prepared by the American delegation to aid in the consideration of the Treaty in its draft form. The notes on the left summarize the contents of the several clauses; those on the right mention points of significance to the American negotiators. The notes are not in every detail the same as those that were attached to the draft Treaty, but in essentials they conform to the original, and they indicate in what way the American economic staff did its work.

ECONOMIC CLAUSES.

SECTION I.

COMMERCIAL RELATIONS.

CHAPTER I.

CUSTOMS REGULATIONS, DUTIES AND RESTRICTIONS.

ARTICLE 264.

Equality of duties for all states.

To cease at end of five years unless League of Nations acts. (See Article 280.)

Germany undertakes that goods the produce or manufacture of any one of the Allied or Associated States imported into German territory, from whatsoever place arriving, shall not be subjected to other or higher duties or charges (including internal charges) than those to which the like goods the produce or manufacture of any other such State or of any other foreign country are subject.

Equality and regulation of imports.

Germany will not maintain or impose any prohibition or restriction on the importation into German territory of any goods the produce or manufacture of the territories of any one of the Allied or Associated States, from whatsoever place arriving, which shall not equally extend to the importation of the like goods the produce or manufacture of any other such State or of any other foreign country.

ARTICLE 265.

No discrimination by indirect methods.

To cease at end of five years unless League of Nations acts. (See Article 280.)

Germany further undertakes that, in the matter of the régime applicable on importation, no discrimination against the commerce of any of the Allied and Associated States as compared with any other of the said States or any other foreign country shall be made, even by indirect means, such as customs regulations or procedure, methods of verification or analysis conditions of payments of duties, tariff classification or interpretation, or the operation of monopolies.

ARTICLE 266.

No discrimination as regards exported goods.

To cease at end of five years unless League of Nations acts. (See Article 280.)

In all that concerns exportation Germany undertakes that goods, natural products or manufactured articles, exported from German territory to the territories of any one of the Allied or Associated States shall not be subjected to other or higher duties or charges (including internal charges) than those paid on the like goods exported to any other such State or to any other foreign country.

Germany will not maintain or impose any prohibition or restriction on the exportation of any goods sent from her territory to any one of the Allied or Associated States which shall not equally extend to the exportation of the like goods, natural products or manufactured articles, sent to any other such state or to any other foreign country.

ARTICLE 267.

All favors to be granted equally.

To cease at end of five years unless League of Nations acts. (See Article 280.)

Every favour, immunity or privilege in regard to the importation, exportation or transit of goods granted by Germany to any Allied or Associated State or to any other foreign country whatever shall simultaneously and unconditionally, without request and without compensation, be extended to all the Allied and Associated States.

ARTICLE 268.

Automatically ends after five years.

The provisions of Articles 264 to 267 inclusive of this Chapter and of Article 323 of Part XII (Ports, Waterways and Railways) of the present Treaty are subject to the following exceptions:

Alsace-Lorraine products free into Germany for five years.

(*a*) For a period of five years from the coming into force of the present Treaty, natural or manufactured products which both originate in and come from the territories of Alsace and Lorraine reunited to France shall, on importation into German customs territory, be exempt from all customs duty.

The French Government shall fix each year, by decree communicated to the German Government, the nature and amount of the products which shall enjoy this exemption.

The amount of each product which may be thus sent annually into Germany shall not exceed the average of the amounts sent annually in the years 1911-1913.

Alsace textiles to move freely for finishing operations.

Automatically ends after five years.

Further, during the period above mentioned the German Government shall allow the free export from Germany and the free re-importation into Germany, exempt from all customs duties and other charges (including internal charges), of yarns, tissues, and other textile materials or textile products of any kind and in any condition, sent from Germany into the territories of Alsace or Lorraine, to be subjected there to any finishing process, such as bleaching, dyeing, printing, mercerisation, gassing, twisting or dressing.

Polish products free into Germany for three years.

Automatically ends after three years.

(*b*) During a period of three years from the coming into force of the present Treaty natural or manufactured products which both originate in and come from Polish territories which before the war were part of Germany, shall, on importation into German customs territory, be exempt from all customs duty.

The Polish Government shall fix each year, by decree communicated to the German Government, the nature and amount of the products which shall enjoy this exemption.

The amount of each product which may be thus sent annually into Germany shall not exceed the average of the amounts sent annually in the years 1911-1913.

Luxemburg case reserved.

Automatically ends after five years.

(*c*) The Allied and Associated Powers reserve the right to require Germany to accord freedom from customs duty, on importation into German customs territory, to natural products and manufactured articles which both originate in and come from the Grand Duchy of Luxemburg, for a period of five years from the coming into force of the present Treaty.

The nature and amount of the products which shall enjoy the benefits of this régime shall be communicated each year to the German Government.

The amount of each product which may be thus sent annually into Germany shall not exceed the average of the amounts sent annually in the years 1911-1913.

Article 269.

Lowest German duties of 1914 to remain in force

During the first six months after the coming into force of the present Treaty,

for six months. Certain other duties to remain unchanged for thirty months more.

the duties imposed by Germany on imports from Allied and Associated States shall not be higher than the most favourable duties which were applied to imports into Germany on July 31, 1914.

A concession to certain countries (especially Italy) who fear the imposition by Germany of vengeful duties on some products dependent particularly on the German market. Automatically ends after three years.

During a further period of thirty months after the expiration of the first six months, this provision shall continue to be applied exclusively with regard to products which, being comprised in Section A of the First Category of the German Customs Tariff of December 25, 1902, enjoyed at the above-mentioned date (July 31, 1914) rates conventionalised by treaties with the Allied and Associated Powers, with the addition of all kinds of wine and vegetable oils, of artificial silk and of washed or scoured wool, whether or not they were the subject of special conventions before July 31, 1914.

ARTICLE 270.

Reservations as to occupied regions.

The Allied and Associated Powers reserve the right to apply to German territory occupied by their troops a special customs régime as regards imports and exports, in the event of such a measure being necessary in their opinion in order to safeguard the economic interests of the population of these territories.

CHAPTER II.

SHIPPING.

ARTICLE 271.

Most-favored-nation treatment for fishing and coasting vessels.

As regards sea fishing, maritime coasting trade, and maritime towage, vessels of the Allied and Associated Powers shall enjoy, in German territorial waters, the treatment accorded to vessels of the most favoured nation.

To cease at end of five years unless League of Nations acts. (See Article 280.)

ARTICLE 272.

Police of North Sea fisheries.

Germany agrees that, notwithstanding any stipulation to the contrary contained in the Conventions relating to the North Sea fisheries and liquor traffic, all rights of inspection and police shall, in the case of fishing-boats of the Allied Powers, be exercised solely by ships belonging to those Powers.

To cease at end of five years unless League of Nations acts. (See Article 280.)

ARTICLE 273.

Ship certificates and documents.

In the case of vessels of the Allied or Associated Powers, all classes of certificates or documents relating to the vessel, which were recognized as valid by Germany before the war, or which may hereafter be recognised as valid by the principal maritime States, shall be recognised by Germany as

Permanent.

valid and as equivalent to the corresponding certificates issued to German vessels.

Permanent.

A similar recognition shall be accorded to the certificates and documents issued to their vessels by the Governments of new States, whether they have a sea-coast or not, provided that such certificates and documents shall be issued in conformity with the general practice observed in the principal maritime States.

Registry of ships of countries having no sea-coast.

Permanent.

The High Contracting Parties agree to recognise the flag flown by the vessels of an Allied or Associated Power having no sea-coast which are registered at some one specified place situated in its territory; such place shall serve as the port of registry of such vessels.

CHAPTER III.

UNFAIR COMPETITION.

ARTICLE 274.

False wrappings and markings to be suppressed by German Government.

This is in accord with the Madrid Convention. The Allies do not here enter on any reciprocal engagement, but the important Allied countries already reciprocate.

Germany undertakes to adopt all the necessary legislative and administrative measures to protect goods the produce or manufacture of any one of the Allied and Associated Powers from all forms of unfair competition in commercial transactions.

Germany undertakes to prohibit and repress by seizure and by other appropriate remedies the importation, exportation, manufacture, distribution, sale or offering for sale in its territory of all goods bearing upon themselves or their usual get-up or wrappings any marks, names, devices, or description whatsoever which are calculated to convey directly or indirectly a false indication of the origin, type, nature, or special characteristics of such goods.

Article 275.

Germany to enforce regional appellation of wines and spirits as settled by other states which act reciprocally in these matters.

This requirement is conditioned on reciprocity.

Germany undertakes on condition that reciprocity is accorded in these matters to respect any law, or any administrative or judicial decision given in conformity with such law, in force in any Allied or Associated State and duly communicated to her by the proper authorities, defining or regulating the right to any regional appellation in respect of wine or spirits produced in the State to which the region belongs, or the conditions under which the use of any such appellation may be permitted; and the importation, exportation, manufacture, distribution, sale or offering for sale of products or articles bearing regional appellations inconsistent with such law or order shall be prohibited by the German Government and repressed by the measures prescribed in the preceding Article.

CHAPTER IV.

TREATMENT OF NATIONALS OF ALLIED AND ASSOCIATED POWERS.

ARTICLE 276.

Germany undertakes:

National treatment in Germany as regards occupations and industry.

To remain in effect five years, with possible prolongation for another five years. (See Article 280.)

(*a*) Not to subject the nationals of the Allied and Associated Powers to any prohibition in regard to the exercise of occupations, professions, trade and industry, which shall not be equally applicable to all aliens without exception;

No indirect evasion.

(*b*) Not to subject the nationals of the Allied and Associated Powers in regard to the rights referred to in paragraph (*a*) to any regulation or restriction which might contravene directly or indirectly the stipulations of the said paragraph, or which shall be other or more disadvantageous than those which are applicable to nationals of the most favoured nation;

National treatment as regards taxes.

(*c*) Not to subject the nationals of the Allied and Associated Powers, their property, rights or interests, including companies and associations in which they are interested, to any charge, tax or impost, direct or indirect, other or higher than those which are or may be imposed on her own nationals or their property, rights or interests;

National treatment in general.

(*d*) Not to subject the nationals of any one of the Allied and Associated Powers to any restriction which was not applicable on July 1, 1914, to the nationals of such Powers unless such restriction is likewise imposed on her own nationals.

ARTICLE 277.

Protection under local laws generally. Permanent.

The nationals of the Allied and Associated Powers shall enjoy in German territory a constant protection for their persons and for their property, rights and interests, and shall have free access to the courts of law.

ARTICLE 278.

Recognition of new nationalities acquired by German and Allied and associated countries. Permanent.

Germany undertakes to recognise any new nationality which has been or may be acquired by her nationals under the laws of the Allied and Associated Powers and in accordance with the decisions of the competent authorities of these Powers pursuant to naturalisation laws or under treaty stipulations, and to regard such persons as having, in consequence of the acquisition of such new nationality, in all respects severed their allegiance to their country of origin.

ARTICLE 279.

Consuls and consular agents to be admitted. Permanent.

The Allied and Associated Powers may appoint consuls-general, consuls, vice-consuls, and consular agents in German towns and ports. Germany undertakes to approve the designation of the consuls-general, consuls, vice-consuls, and consular agents, whose names shall be notified to her, and to admit them to the exercise of their functions in conformity with the usual rules and customs.

Chapter V.

GENERAL ARTICLES.

Article 280.

Period of time during which certain of the preceding obligations shall remain in effect.

The obligations imposed on Germany by Chapter I and by Articles 271 and 272 of Chapter II above shall cease to have effect five years from the date of the coming into force of the present Treaty, unless otherwise provided in the text, or unless the Council of the League of Nations shall, at least twelve months before the expiration of that period, decide that these obligations shall be maintained for a further period with or without amendment.

Article 276 of Chapter IV shall remain in operation, with or without amendment, after the period of five years for such further period, if any, not exceeding five years, as may be determined by a majority of the Council of the League of Nations.

ARTICLE 281.

German Government, when acting as a trader, to have no immunity as a sovereign.

If the German Government engages in international trade, it shall not in respect thereof have or be deemed to have any rights, privileges or immunities of sovereignty.

SECTION II.

TREATIES.

ARTICLE 282.

From the coming into force of the present Treaty and subject to the provisions thereof the multilateral treaties, conventions and agreements of an economic or technical character enumerated below and in the subsequent Articles shall alone be applied as between Germany and those of the Allied and Associated Powers party thereto:

Relations re-established in respect of multilateral conventions and international unions.

U. S. a party.

(1) Conventions of March 14, 1884, December 1, 1886, and March 23, 1887, and Final Protocol of July 7, 1887, regarding the protection of submarine cables.

European.

(2) Convention of October 11, 1909, regarding the international circulation of motor-cars.

European.

(3) Agreement of May 15, 1886, regarding the sealing of railway trucks subject to customs inspection, and Protocol of May 18, 1907.

(4) Agreement of May 15, 1886, regarding the technical standardisation of railways.

European.

(5) Convention of July 5, 1890, regarding the publication of customs tariffs and the organisation of an International Union for the publication of customs tariffs.

U. S. a party.

(6) Convention of December 31, 1913, regarding the unification of commercial statistics.

European.

(7) Convention of April 25, 1907, regarding the raising of the Turkish customs tariff.

European.

(8) Convention of March 14, 1857, for the redemption of toll dues on the Sound and Belts.

U. S. a party.

(9) Convention of June 22, 1861, for the redemption of the State Toll on the Elbe.

European.

(10) Convention of July 16, 1863, for the redemption of the toll dues on the Scheldt.

European.

(11) Convention of October 29, 1888, regarding the establishment of a definite arrangement guaranteeing the free use of the Suez Canal.

(12) Convention of September 23, 1910, respecting the unification of certain regulations regarding collisions and salvage at sea.

U. S. a party to the salvage convention treaty only.

(13) Convention of December 21, 1904, regarding the exemption of hospital ships from dues and charges in ports. European.

(14) Convention of February 4, 1898, regarding the tonnage measurement of vessels for inland navigation. European.

(15) Convention of September 26, 1906, for the suppression of night work for women. European.

(16) Convention of September 26, 1906, for the suppression of the use of white phosphorus in the manufacture of matches. U. S. a party.

(17) Conventions of May 18, 1904, and May 4, 1910, regarding the suppression of the White Slave Traffic. U. S. a party.

(18) Convention of May 4, 1910, regarding the suppression of obscene publications. U. S. a party.

(19) Sanitary Conventions of January 30, 1892, April 15, 1893, April 3, 1894, March 19, 1897, and December 3, 1903. U. S. a party.

(20) Convention of May 20, 1875, regarding the unification and improvement of the metric system. European.

(21) Convention of November 29, 1906, regarding the unification of pharmacopœial formulæ for potent drugs. European.

(22) Convention of November 16 and 19, 1885, regarding the establishment of a concert pitch. U. S. a party.

(23) Convention of June 7, 1905, regarding the creation of an International Agricultural Institute at Rome.

European.

(24) Conventions of November 3, 1881, and April 15, 1889, regarding precautionary measures against phylloxera.

European.

(25) Convention of March 19, 1902, regarding the protection of birds useful to agriculture.

U. S. not a party.

(26) Convention of June 12, 1902, as to the protection of minors.

ARTICLE 283.

From the coming into force of the present Treaty the High Contracting Parties shall apply the conventions and agreements hereinafter mentioned, in so far as concerns them, on condition that the special stipulations contained in this Article are fulfilled by Germany.

Postal Conventions:

Conventions and agreements of the Universal Postal Union concluded at Vienna, July 4, 1891.

U. S. a party.

Conventions and agreements of the Postal Union signed at Washington, June 15, 1897.

Conventions and agreements of the Postal Union signed at Rome, May 26, 1906.

Telegraphic Conventions:

International Telegraphic Conventions signed at St. Petersburg July 10-22, 1875.

U. S. not a party.

Regulations and Tariffs drawn up by the International Telegraphic Conference, Lisbon, June 11, 1908.

U. S. not a party.

Germany to conclude reciprocal postal and telegraphic agreements with the new states.

Germany undertakes not to refuse her assent to the conclusion by the new States of the special arrangements referred to in the conventions and agreements relating to the Universal Postal Union and to the International Telegraphic Union, to which the said new States have adhered or may adhere.

ARTICLE 284.

Application of Radio-Telegraphic convention.

U. S. a party.

From the coming into force of the present Treaty the High Contracting Parties shall apply, in so far as concerns them, the International Radio-Telegraphic Convention of July 5, 1912, on condition that Germany fulfils the provisional regulations which will be indicated to her by the Allied and Associated Powers.

Germany to be bound by possible new radio-telegraphic convention.

Alleged to be necessary for military reasons.

If within five years after the coming into force of the present Treaty a new convention regulating international radio-telegraphic communications should have been concluded to take the place of the Convention of July 5, 1912, this new convention shall bind Germany, even if Germany should refuse either to take part in drawing up the convention, or to subscribe thereto.

This new convention will likewise replace the provisional regulations in force.

ARTICLE 285.

From the coming into force of the present Treaty, the High Contracting Parties shall apply in so far as concerns them and under the conditions stipulated in Article 272, the conventions hereinafter mentioned:

Revival of North Sea fisheries convention.

(1) The Conventions of May 6, 1882, and February 1, 1889, regulating the fisheries in the North Sea outside territorial waters.

European.

Revival of North Sea liquor traffic convention.

(2) The Conventions and Protocols of November 16, 1887, February 14, 1893, and April 11, 1894, regarding the North Sea liquor traffic.

European.

ARTICLE 286.

Revival of International Conventions covering patents, trade-marks, and copyrights.

The International Convention of Paris of March 20, 1883, for the protection of industrial property, revised at Washington on June 2, 1911; and the International Convention of Berne of September 9, 1886, for the protection of literary and artistic works, revised at Berlin on November 13, 1908, and completed by the additional Protocol signed at Berne on March 20, 1914, will again come

U. S. a party.

into effect as from the coming into force of the present Treaty, in so far as they are not affected or modified by the exceptions and restrictions resulting therefrom.

ARTICLE 287.

Renewal of Convention relating to civil procedure.

European.

From the coming into force of the present Treaty the High Contracting Parties shall apply, in so far as concerns them, the Convention of The Hague of July 17, 1905, relating to civil procedure. This renewal, however, will not apply to France, Portugal and Roumania.

ARTICLE 288.

National treatment of German trade in Samoa to terminate.

These rights, granted by U. S. and Great Britain, were incidental to the Samoan adjustment of 1899.

The special rights and privileges granted to Germany by Article 3 of the Convention of December 2, 1899, relating to Samoa shall be considered to have terminated on August 4, 1914.

ARTICLE 289.

Revival of bilateral treaties with Germany, in whole or in part, upon notification by Allied or Associated Powers.

Each of the Allied or Associated Powers, being guided by the general principles or special provisions of the present Treaty, shall notify to Germany the bilateral treaties or conventions which such Allied or Associated Power wishes to revive with Germany.

The notification referred to in the present Article shall be made either directly or through the intermediary of another Power. Receipt thereof shall be acknowledged in writing by Germany. The date of the revival shall be that of the notification.

Allied and Associated Powers agree not to revive conventions or treaties not in accord with present Treaty.

The Allied and Associated Powers undertake among themselves not to revive with Germany any conventions or treaties which are not in accordance with the terms of the present Treaty.

The notification shall mention any provisions of the said conventions and treaties which, not being in accordance with the terms of the present Treaty, shall not be considered as revived.

In case of any difference of opinion, the League of Nations will be called on to decide.

Six months' time limit on notification.

A period of six months from the coming into force of the present Treaty is allowed to the Allied and Associated Powers within which to make the notification.

Bilateral treaties and conventions not thus revived remain abrogated.

Only those bilateral treaties and conventions which have been the subject of such a notification shall be revived between the Allied and Associated Powers and Germany; all the others are and shall remain abrogated.

Although the Allied Powers decide what treaties shall be revived, by the terms of these treaties Germany will still be able to renounce most of them by giving twelve months' notice.

The above regulations apply to all bilateral treaties or conventions existing between all the Allied and Associated Powers signatories to the present Treaty and Germany, even if the said Allied and Associated Powers have not been in a state of war with Germany.

ARTICLE 290.

Enemy treaties entered into during the War are abrogated by this clause.

Germany recognizes that all the treaties, conventions or agreements which she has concluded with Austria, Hungary, Bulgaria or Turkey since August 1, 1914, until the coming into force of the present Treaty are and remain abrogated by the present Treaty.

ARTICLE 291.

Most-favored-nation treatment under pre-War enemy treaties.

Germany undertakes to secure to the Allied and Associated Powers, and to the officials and nationals of the said Powers, the enjoyment of all the rights and advantages of any kind which she may have granted to Austria, Hungary, Bulgaria or Turkey, or to the officials and nationals of these States by treaties, conventions or arrangements concluded before August 1, 1914, so long as those treaties, conventions or arrangements remain in force.

The Allied and Associated Powers reserve the right to accept or not the enjoyment of these rights and advantages.

ARTICLE 292.

Enemy treaties with Russia and

This abrogates all German

Germany recognizes that all treaties, conventions or arrangements which she con-

Roumania abrogated.

cluded with Russia, or with any State or Government of which the territory previously formed a part of Russia, or with Roumania, before August 1, 1914, or after that date until coming into force of the present Treaty, are and remain abrogated.

treaties with Finland, as well as with the Ukraine.

Article 293.

Annuls concessions, etc., granted under pressure to Germany by Russia or states formerly constituting a part of Russia.

Should an Allied or Associated Power, Russia, or a State or Government of which the territory formerly constituted a part of Russia, have been forced since August 1, 1914, by reason of military occupation or by any other means or for any other cause, to grant or to allow to be granted by the act of any public authority, concessions, privileges and favours of any kind to Germany or to a German national, such concessions, privileges and favours are *ipso facto* annulled by the present Treaty.

No claims or indemnities which may result from this annulment shall be charged against the Allied or Associated Powers or the Powers, States, Governments or public authorities which are released from their engagements by the present Article.

Article 294

Allied and Associated Powers to receive benefits of German treaties concluded with neutrals.

From the coming into force of the present Treaty Germany undertakes to give the Allied and Associated Powers and their nationals the benefit *ipso facto* of the rights and advantages of any kind which she has granted by treaties, conventions, or arrangements to non-belligerent States or their nationals since August 1, 1914, until the coming into force of the present Treaty, so long as those treaties, conventions or arrangements remain in force.

ARTICLE 295.

General participation of contracting parties in opium treaty of 1912.

Already signed but not ratified by Germany.

Those of the High Contracting Parties who have not yet signed, or who have signed but not yet ratified, the Opium Convention signed at The Hague on January 23, 1912, agree to bring the said Convention into force, and for this purpose to enact the necessary legislation without delay and in any case within a period of twelve months from the coming into force of the present Treaty.

Furthermore, they agree that ratification of the present Treaty should in the case of Powers which have not yet ratified the Opium Convention be deemed in all respects equivalent to the ratification of that Convention and to the signature of the Special Protocol which was opened at The Hague in accordance with the resolutions adopted by the Third Opium Conference in 1914 for bringing the said Convention into force.

For this purpose the Government of the French Republic will communicate to the Government of the Netherlands a certified copy of the protocol of the deposit of ratifications of the present Treaty, and will invite the Government of the Netherlands to accept and deposit the said certified copy as if it were a deposit of ratifications of the Opium Convention and a signature of the Additional Protocol of 1914.

SECTION III.

DEBTS.

ARTICLE 296.

There shall be settled through the intervention of clearing offices to be established by each of the High Contracting Parties within three months of the notification referred to in paragraph (*e*) hereafter the following classes of pecuniary obligations:

Provides for clearing-house system for the collection of debts, and the use of proceeds of enemy property.

(1) Debts payable before the war and due by a national of one of the Contracting Powers, residing within its territory, to a national of an Opposing Power, residing within its territory;

Optional and not expected to be adopted by U. S. (See paragraph 4(*e*) of this article.)

(2) Debts which became payable during the war to nationals of one Contracting Power residing within its territory and arose out of the transactions or contracts with the nationals of an Opposing Power, resident within its territory, of which the total or partial execution was suspended on account of the declaration of war;

(3) Interest which has accrued due before and during the war to a national of one of the Contracting Powers in respect of securities issued by an Opposing Power, provided that the payment of interest on such securities to the nationals of that Power or to neutrals has not been suspended during the war;

(4) Capital sums which have become payable before and during the war to nationals of one of the Contracting Powers in respect of securities issued by one of the Opposing Powers, provided that the payment of such capital sums to nationals of that Power or to neutrals has not been suspended during the war.

The proceeds of liquidation of enemy property, rights and interests mentioned in Section IV and in the Annex thereto will be accounted for through the Clearing Offices, in the currency and at the rate of exchange hereinafter provided in paragraph (*d*), and disposed of by them under the conditions provided by the said Section and Annex.

The settlements provided for in this Article shall be effected according to the following principles and in accordance with the Annex to this Section:

Prohibits Allied and enemy nationals from settling their debts with each other, or even from

(*a*) Each of the High Contracting Parties shall prohibit, as from the coming into force of the present Treaty, both the payment and the acceptance of payment of such

communicating with each other about them.

debts, and also all communications between the interested parties with regard to the settlement of the said debts otherwise than through the Clearing Offices;

Requires each Government to guarantee the payment of debts owed by its nationals to former enemy nationals.

(*b*) Each of the High Contracting Parties shall be respectively responsible for the payment of such debts due by its nationals, except in the cases where before the war the debtor was in a state of bankruptcy or failure, or had given formal indication of insolvency or where the debt was due by a company whose business has been liquidated under emergency legislation during the war. Nevertheless, debts due by the inhabitants of territory invaded or occupied by the enemy before the Armistice will not be guaranteed by the States of which those territories form part;

(*c*) The sums due to the nationals of one of the High Contracting Parties by the nationals of an Opposing State will be debited to the Clearing Office of the country of the debtor, and paid to the creditor by the Clearing Office of the country of the creditor;

Rate of exchange in settlement of debt.

(*d*) Debts shall be paid or credited in the currency of such one of the Allied and Associated Powers, their colonies or protectorates, or the British Dominions or India, as may be concerned. If the debts are payable in some other currency they shall be paid or credited in the currency of the country concerned, whether an Allied or Associated Power, Colony, Protectorate, British Dominion or India, at the pre-war rate of exchange.

For the purpose of this provision the pre-war rate of exchange shall be defined as the average cable transfer rate prevailing in the Allied or Associated country concerned during the month immediately preceding the outbreak of war between the said country concerned and Germany.

If a contract provides for a fixed rate of exchange governing the conversion of the currency in which the debt is stated into the currency of the Allied or Associated country concerned, then the above provisions concerning the rate of exchange shall not apply.

In the case of new States the currency in which and the rate of exchange at which debts shall be paid or credited shall be determined by the Reparation Commission provided for in Part VIII (Reparation);

Does not apply to any Allied state unless adopted by it within one month after ratification.

(*e*) The provisions of this Article and of the Annex hereto shall not apply as between Germany on the one hand and any one of the Allied and Associated Powers, their colonies or protectorates, or any one of the British Dominions or India on the other hand, unless within a period of one month from the deposit of the ratification of the

It was expected that the U. S. would avail itself of this clause and keep out of the clearing-house system.

present Treaty by the Power in question, or of the ratification on behalf of such Dominion or of India, notice to that effect is given to Germany by the Government of such Allied or Associated Power or of such Dominion or of India as the case may be;

(*f*) The Allied and Associated Powers who have adopted this Article and the Annex hereto may agree between themselves to apply them to their respective nationals established in their territory so far as regards matters between their nationals and German nationals. In this case the payments made by the application of this provision will be subject to arrangements between the Allied and Associated Clearing Offices concerned.

ANNEX.

1.

Each of the High Contracting Parties will, within three months from the notification provided for in Article 296, paragraph (*e*), establish a Clearing Office for the collection and payment of enemy debts.

The details in this Annex relating generally to procedure do not concern the U. S., which is not expected to adopt the system.

Local Clearing Offices may be established for any particular portion of the territories of the High Contracting Parties. Such local Clearing Offices may perform all the functions of a central Clearing Office in their respective districts, except that all transactions with the Clearing Office in the Opposing State must be effected through the central Clearing Office.

2.

In this Annex the pecuniary obligations referred to in the first paragraph of Article 296 are described as "enemy debts," the persons from whom the same are due as "enemy debtors," the persons to whom they are due as "enemy creditors," the Clearing Office in the country of the creditor is called the "Creditor Clearing Office," and the Clearing Office in the country of the debtor is called the "Debtor Clearing Office."

3.

The High Contracting Parties will subject contraventions of paragraph (*a*) of Article 296 to the same penalties as are at present provided by their legislation for trading with the enemy. They will similarly prohibit within their territory all legal process relating to payment of enemy debts, except in accordance with the provisions of this Annex.

4.

The Government guarantee specified in paragraph (*b*) of Article 296 shall take effect whenever, for any reason, a debt shall not be recoverable, except in a case where at the date of the outbreak of war the debt was barred by the laws of prescription in force in the country of the debtor, or where the debtor was at that time in a state of bankruptcy or failure or had given formal indication of insolvency, or where the debt was due by a company whose business has been liquidated under emergency legislation during the war. In such case the procedure specified by this Annex shall apply to payment of the dividends.

The terms "bankruptcy" and "failure" refer to the application of legislation providing for such juridical conditions. The expression "formal indication of insolvency" bears the same meaning as it has in English law.

5.

Creditors shall give notice to the Creditor Clearing Office within six months of its establishment of debts due to them, and shall furnish the Clearing Office with any documents and information required of them.

The High Contracting Parties will take all suitable measures to trace and punish collusion between enemy creditors and debtors. The Clearing Office will communicate to one another any evidence and information which might help the discovery and punishment of such collusion.

The High Contracting Parties will facilitate as much as possible postal and telegraphic communication at the expense of the parties concerned and through the intervention of the Clearing Offices between debtors and creditors desirous of coming to an agreement as to the amount of their debt.

The Creditor Clearing Office will notify the Debtor Clearing Office of all debts declared to it. The Debtor Clearing Office will, in due course, inform the Creditor Clearing Office which debts are admitted and which debts are contested. In the latter case, the Debtor Clearing Office will give the grounds for the non-admission of debt.

6.

When a debt has been admitted, in whole or in part, the Debtor Clearing Office will at once credit the Creditor Clearing Office with the amount admitted, and at the same time notify it of such credit.

7.

The debt shall be deemed to be admitted in full and shall be credited forthwith to the Creditor Clearing Office unless within three months from the receipt of the notification or such longer time as may be agreed to by the Creditor Clearing Office notice has been given by the Debtor Clearing Office that it is not admitted.

8.

When the whole or part of a debt is not admitted the two Clearing Offices will examine into the matter jointly and will endeavour to bring the parties to an agreement.

9.

The Creditor Clearing Office will pay to the individual creditor the sum credited to it out of the funds placed at its disposal by the Government of its country and in accordance with the conditions fixed by the said Government, retaining any sums considered necessary to cover risks, expenses or commissions.

10.

Any person having claimed payment of an enemy debt which is not admitted in whole or in part shall pay to the clearing office, by way of fine, interest at 5 per cent. on the part not admitted. Any person having unduly refused to admit the whole or part of a debt claimed from him shall pay, by way of fine, interest at 5 per cent. on the amount with regard to which his refusal shall be disallowed.

Such interest shall run from the date of expiration of the period provided for in paragraph 7 until the date on which the claim shall have been disallowed or the debt paid.

Each Clearing Office shall in so far as it is concerned take steps to collect the fines above provided for, and will be responsible if such fines cannot be collected.

The fines will be credited to the other Clearing Office, which shall retain them as a contribution towards the cost of carrying out the present provisions.

11.

The balance between the Clearing Offices shall be struck monthly and the credit balance paid in cash by the debtor State within a week.

Nevertheless, any credit balances which may be due by one or more of the Allied and Associated Powers shall be retained until complete payment shall have been effected of the sums due to the Allied or Associated Powers or their nationals on account of the war.

12.

To facilitate discussion between the Clearing Offices each of them shall have a representative at the place where the other is established.

13.

Except for special reasons all discussions in regard to claims will, so far as possible, take place at the Debtor Clearing Office.

14.

In conformity with Article 296, paragraph (*b*), the High Contracting Parties are responsible for the payment of the enemy debts owing by their nationals.

The Debtor Clearing Office will therefore credit the Creditor Clearing Office with all debts admitted, even in case of inability to collect them from the individual debtor. The Governments concerned will, nevertheless, invest their respective Clearing Offices with all necessary powers for the recovery of debts which have been admitted.

As an exception, the admitted debts owing by persons having suffered injury from acts of war shall only be credited to the Creditor Clearing Office when the compensation due to the person concerned in respect of such injury shall have been paid.

15.

Each Government will defray the expenses of the Clearing Office set up in its territory, including the salaries of the staff.

16.

Where the two Clearing Offices are unable to agree whether a debt claimed is due, or in case of a difference between an enemy debtor and an enemy creditor or between the Clearing Offices, the dispute shall either be referred to arbitration if the parties so agree under conditions fixed by agreement between them, or referred to the Mixed Arbitral Tribunal provided for in Section VI hereafter.

At the request of the Creditor Clearing Office the dispute may, however, be submitted to the jurisdiction of the Courts of the place of domicile of the debtor.

17.

Recovery of sums found by the Mixed Arbitral Tribunal, the Court, or the Arbitration Tribunal to be due shall be effected through the Clearing Offices as if these sums were debts admitted by the Debtor Clearing Office.

18.

Each of the Governments concerned shall appoint an agent who will be responsible for the presentation to the Mixed Arbitral Tribunal of the cases conducted on behalf of its Clearing Office. This agent will exercise a general control over the representatives or counsel employed by its nationals.

Decisions will be arrived at on documentary evidence, but it will be open to the Tribunal to hear the parties in person, or according to their preference by their representatives approved by the two Governments or by the agent referred to above, who shall be competent to intervene along with the party or to reopen and maintain a claim abandoned by the same.

19.

The Clearing Offices concerned will lay before the Mixed Arbitral Tribunal all the information and documents in their possession, so as to enable the Tribunal to decide rapidly on the cases which are brought before it.

20.

Where one of the parties concerned appeals against the joint decision of the two Clearing Offices he shall make a deposit against the costs, which deposit shall only be refunded when the first judgment is modified in favour of the appellant and in proportion to the success he may attain, his opponent in case of such a refund being required to pay an equivalent proportion of the costs and expenses. Security accepted by the Tribunal may be substituted for a deposit.

A fee of 5 per cent. of the amount in dispute shall be charged in respect of all cases brought before the Tribunal. This fee shall, unless the Tribunal directs otherwise, be borne by the unsuccessful party. Such fee shall be added to the deposit referred to. It is also independent of the security.

The Tribunal may award to one of the parties a sum in respect of the expenses of the proceedings.

Any sum payable under this paragraph shall be credited to the Clearing Office of the successful party as a separate item.

21.

With a view to the rapid settlement of claims, due regard shall be paid in the appointment of all persons connected with the Clearing Offices or with the Mixed Arbitral Tribunal to their knowledge of the language of the other country concerned.

Each of the Clearing Offices will be at liberty to correspond with the other and to forward documents in its own language.

22.

Subject to any special agreement to the contrary between the Governments concerned, debts shall carry interest in accordance with the following provisions:

Interest shall not be payable on sums of money due by way of dividend, interest or other periodical payments which themselves represent interest in capital.

The rate of interest shall be 5 per cent. per annum except in cases where, by contract, law or custom, the creditor is entitled to payment of interest at a different rate. In such cases the rate to which he is entitled shall prevail.

Interest shall run from the date of commencement of hostilities (or, if the sum of money to be recovered fell due during the war, from the date at which it fell due) until the sum is credited to the Clearing Office of the creditor.

Sums due by way of interest shall be treated as debts admitted by the Clearing Office and shall be credited to the Creditor Clearing Office in the same way as such debts.

23.

Where by decision of the Clearing Offices or the Mixed Arbitral Tribunal a claim is held not to fall within Article 296, the creditor shall be at liberty to prosecute the claim before the Courts or to take such other proceedings as may be open to him.

The presentation of a claim to the Clearing Office suspends the operation of any period of prescription.

24.

The High Contracting Parties agree to regard the decisions of the Mixed Arbitral Tribunal as final and conclusive, and to render them binding upon their nationals.

25.

In any case where a Creditor Clearing Office declines to notify a claim to the Debtor Clearing Office, or to take any step provided for in this Annex, intended to make effective in whole or in part a request of which it has received due notice, the enemy creditor shall be entitled to receive from the Clearing Office a certificate setting out the amount of the claim, and shall then be entitled to prosecute the claim before the courts or to take such other proceedings as may be open to him.

Section IV.

PROPERTY, RIGHTS AND INTERESTS.

Article 297.

The question of private property, rights and interests in an enemy country shall be settled according to the principles laid down in this Section and to the provisions of the Annex hereto.

Requires the restoration of Allied property in Germany not **already sold.**

(*a*) The exceptional war measures and measures of transfer (defined in paragraph 3 of the Annex hereto) taken by Germany with respect to the property, rights and interests of nationals of Allied or Associated Powers, including companies and associations in which they are interested, when liquidation has not been completed, shall be immediately discontinued or stayed and the property, rights and interests concerned restored to their owners, who shall enjoy full rights therein in accordance with the provisions of Article 298.

Authorizes the Allies to sell in future German property in their territory, at their option.

(*b*) Subject to any contrary stipulations which may be provided for in the present Treaty, the Allied and Associated Powers reserve the right to retain and liquidate all property, rights and interests belonging at the date of the coming into force of the present Treaty to German nationals, or companies controlled by them, within their territories, colonies, possessions and protectorates, including territory ceded to them by the present Treaty.

German owner shall not dispose of such property without consent of State interested.

The liquidation shall be carried out in accordance with the laws of the Allied or Associated State concerned, and the German owner shall not be able to dispose of such property, rights or interests nor to subject them to any charge without the consent of that State.

German nationals who acquire *ipso facto* the nationality of an Allied or Associated Power in accordance with the provisions of the present Treaty will not be considered as German nationals within the meaning of this paragraph.

The prices and valuations for future sales in Allied countries will be fixed by the laws of such countries.

(*c*) The price or the amount of compensation in respect of the exercise of the right referred to in the preceding paragraph (*b*) will be fixed in accordance with the methods of sale or valuation adopted by the laws of the country in which the property has been retained or liquidated.

As between Allies and Germany all sales and actions heretofore taken under exceptional war measures are confirmed.

(*d*) As between the Allied and Associated Powers or their nationals on the one hand and Germany or her nationals on the other hand, all the exceptional war measures, or measures of transfer, or acts done or to be done in execution of such measures as defined in paragraphs 1 and 3 of the Annex hereto shall be considered as final and binding upon all persons except as regards the reservations laid down in the present Treaty.

Claims of Allied citizens for injuries to their property in Germany to be passed upon

(*e*) The nationals of Allied and Associated Powers shall be entitled to compensation in respect of damage or injury inflicted upon their property, rights or interests, in-by a mixed court with a neutral president. Such claims shall be assumed by Germany, and may be paid by Allied states out of German property in their hands.

cluding any company or association in which they are interested, in German territory as it existed on August 1, 1914, by the application either of the exceptional war measures or measures of transfer mentioned in paragraphs 1 and 3 of the Annex hereto. The claims made in this respect by such nationals shall be investigated, and the total of the compensation shall be determined by the Mixed Arbitral Tribunal provided for in Section VI or by an Arbitrator appointed by that Tribunal. This compensation shall be borne by Germany, and may be charged upon the property of German nationals within the territory or under the control of the claimant's State. This property may be constituted as a pledge for enemy liabilities under the conditions fixed by paragraph 4 of the Annex hereto. The payment of this compensation may be made by the Allied or Associated State, and the amount will be debited to Germany.

Requires the restoration of property sold, but, under (*g*), applies only to countries which have not sold German property.

Does not apply to U. S.

(*f*) Whenever a national of an Allied or Associated Power is entitled to property which has been subjected to a measure of transfer in German territory and expresses a desire for its restitution, his claim for compensation in accordance with paragraph (*e*) shall be satisfied by the restitution of the said property if it still exists in specie.

In such case Germany shall take all necessary steps to restore the evicted owner to the possession of his property, free from all encumbrances or burdens with which it may have been charged after the liquidation, and to indemnify all third parties injured by the restitution.

If the restitution provided for in this paragraph cannot be effected, private agreements arranged by the intermediation of the Powers concerned or the Clearing Offices provided for in the Annex to Section III may be made, in order to secure that the national of the Allied or Associated Power may secure compensation for the injury referred to in paragraph (*e*) by the grant of advantages or equivalents which he agrees to accept in place of the property, rights or interests of which he was deprived.

Through restitution in accordance with this Article, the price or the amount of compensation fixed by the application of paragraph (*e*) will be reduced by the actual value of the property restored, account being taken of compensation in respect of loss of use or deterioration.

(*g*) The rights conferred by paragraph (*f*) are reserved to owners who are nationals of Allied or Associated Powers within whose territory legislative measures prescribing the general liquidation of enemy property, rights or interests were not applied before the signature of the Armistice.

(*h*) Except in cases where, by application of paragraph (*f*), restitutions in specie have been made, the net proceeds of sales of enemy property, rights or interests wherever situated carried out either by virtue of war legislation, or by application of this Article, and in general all cash assets of enemies, shall be dealt with as follows:

General rules for disposition of proceeds of enemy property.

The U. S. does not expect to adopt Section III.

(1) As regards Powers adopting Section III and the Annex thereto, the said proceeds and cash assets shall be credited to the Power of which the owner is a national, through the Clearing Office established thereunder; any credit balance in favour of Germany resulting therefrom shall be dealt with as provided in Article 243.

Proceeds of property, &c., cash assets of Allied nationals held by Germany to be paid immediately to said national or his Government.

Concerns U. S. if Section III is not adopted.

(2) As regards Powers not adopting Section III and the Annex thereto, the proceeds of the property, rights and interests, and the cash assets, of the nationals of Allied or Associated Powers held by Germany shall be paid immediately to the person entitled thereto or to his Government; the proceeds of the property, rights and interests, and the cash assets, of German nationals received by an Allied or Associated Power shall be subject to disposal by such Power in accordance with its laws and regulations and may be applied in payment of the claims and debts

Like proceeds of German nationals to be at disposal of Allied Powers and may be applied to payment claims and debts defined by this Article.

defined by this Article or paragraph 4 of the Annex hereto. Any property, rights and interests or proceeds thereof or cash assets not used as above provided may be retained by the said Allied or Associated Power and if retained the cash value thereof shall be dealt with as provided in Article 243.

Exceptional treatment of enemy property in new states.

In the case of liquidations effected in new States, which are signatories of the present Treaty as Allied and Associated Powers, or in States which are not entitled to share in the reparation payments to be made by Germany, the proceeds of liquidations effected by such States shall, subject to the rights of the Reparation Commission under the present Treaty, particularly under Articles 235 and 260, be paid direct to the owner. If on application of that owner, the Mixed Arbitral Tribunal, provided for by Section VI of this Part, or an arbitrator appointed by that Tribunal, is satisfied that the conditions of the sale or measures taken by the Government of the State in question outside its general legislation were unfairly prejudicial to the price obtained, they shall have discretion to award to the owner equitable compensation to be paid by that State.

Requires Germany to pay its own nationals for

(*i*) Germany undertakes to compensate her nationals in respect of the sale or retheir property if taken by Allied states.

tention of their property, rights or interests in Allied or Associated States.

Taxes and imposts levied by Germany from Nov. 11, 1918, and up to three months after coming into force of Treaty to be restored. Also property, &c., subjected to exceptional war measures during that period.

(*j*) The amount of all taxes and imposts upon capital levied or to be levied by Germany on the property, rights and interests of the nationals of the Allied or Associated Powers from November 11, 1918, until three months from the coming into force of the present Treaty, or, in the case of property, rights or interests which have been subjected to exceptional measures of war, until restitution in accordance with the present Treaty shall be restored to the owners.

Article 298.

Germany undertakes, with regard to the property, rights and interests, including companies and associations in which they were interested, restored to nationals of Allied and Associated Powers in accordance with the provisions of Article 297, paragraph (*a*) or (*f*):

Property, &c., restored by Germany to have same legal status as property of German nationals before the war.

(*a*) to restore and maintain, except as expressly provided in the present Treaty, the property, rights and interests of the nationals of Allied or Associated Powers in the legal position obtaining in respect of the property, rights and interests of German nationals under the laws in force before the war;

Germany agrees not to discriminate against Allied nationals in treatment of their property, and to pay compensation if measures are taken in derogation of it.

(*b*) not to subject the property, rights or interests of the nationals of the Allied or Associated Powers to any measures in derogation of property rights which are not applied equally to the property, rights and interests of German nationals, and to pay adequate compensation in the event of the application of these measures.

ANNEX.

1.

Merely amplifies Art. 297 (*d*); applies to all countries alike, including Germany.

Important for U. S., as it validates action of Alien Property Custodian, so far as German Government is concerned.

In accordance with the provisions of Article 297, paragraph (*d*), the validity of vesting orders and of orders for the winding up of businesses or companies, and of any other orders, directions, decisions or instructions of any court or any department of the Government of any of the High Contracting Parties made or given, or purporting to be made or given, in pursuance of war legislation with regard to enemy property, rights and interests is confirmed. The interests of all persons shall be regarded as having been effectively dealt with by any order, direction, decision or instruction dealing with property in which they may be interested, whether or not such interests are specifically mentioned in the order, direction, decision, or instruction. No question shall be raised as to the regularity of a transfer of any property, rights or interests dealt with in pursuance of any such order, direction, decision or instruction. Every action taken with regard to any property, business, or company, whether as regards its investigation, sequestration, compulsory administration, use, requisition, supervision, or winding up, the sale or management of property, rights or interests, the collection or discharge of debts, the payment of costs, charges or expenses, or any other matter whatsoever, in pursuance of orders, directions, decisions, or instructions of any court or of any department of the Government of any of the High Contracting Parties, made or given, or purporting to be made or given, in pursuance of war legislation with regard to enemy property, rights or interests, is confirmed. Provided that the provisions of this paragraph shall not be held to prejudice the titles to property heretofore acquired in good faith and for value and in accordance with the laws of the country in which the property is situated by nationals of the Allied and Associated Powers.

This proviso preserves rights of our citizens who bought property of Germans in good faith before we entered the War.

The provisions of this paragraph do not apply to such of the above-mentioned measures as have been taken by the German authorities in invaded or occupied territory, nor to such of the above mentioned measures as have been taken by Germany or the

German authorities since November 11, 1918, all of which shall be void.

2.

Prevents claims being brought by Germany or its nationals on account of War measures.

No claim or action shall be made or brought against any Allied or Associated Power or against any person acting on behalf of or under the direction of any legal authority or Department of the Government of such a Power by Germany or by any German national wherever resident in respect of any act or omission with regard to his property, rights or interests during the war or in preparation for the war. Similarly no claim or action shall be made or brought against any person in respect of any act or omission under or in accordance with the exceptional war measures, laws or regulations of any Allied or Associated Power.

Intended to prevent claims on account of operation of our War legislation, *e. g.*, black list of War Trade Board.

3.

Merely defines the terms used.

In Article 297 and this Annex the expression "exceptional war measures" includes measures of all kinds, legislative, administrative, judicial or others, that have been taken or will be taken hereafter with regard to enemy property, and which have had or will have the effect of removing from the proprietors the power of disposition over their property, though without affecting the ownership, such as measures of supervision, of compulsory administration, and of sequestration; or measures which have had or will have as an object the seizure of, the use of, or the interference with enemy assets, for whatsoever motive, under whatsoever form or in whatsoever place. Acts in the execution of these measures include all detentions, instructions, orders or decrees of Government departments or courts applying these measures to enemy property, as well as acts performed by any person connected with the administration or the supervision of enemy property, such as the payment of debts, the collecting of credits, the payment of any costs, charges or expenses, or the collecting of fees.

Measures of transfer are those which have affected or will affect the ownership of enemy property by transferring it in whole or in part to a person other than the enemy owner, and without his consent, such as measures directing the sale, liquidation, or devolution of ownership in enemy property, or the cancelling of titles or securities.

4.

Classes of claims for payment of which German property may be used by Allied and Associated Powers.

All property, rights and interests of German nationals within the territory of any Allied or Associated Power and the net proceeds of their sale, liquidation or other dealings therewith may be charged by that Allied or Associated Power in the first place with payment of amounts due in respect of claims by the nationals of that Allied or Associated Power with regard to their property, rights and interests, including companies and associations in which they are interested, in German territory, or debts owing to them by German nationals, and with payment of claims growing out of acts committed by the German Government or by any German authorities since July 31, 1914, and before that Allied or Associated Power entered into the war. The amount of such claims may be assessed by an arbitrator appointed by M. Gustave Ador, if he is willing, or if no such appointment is made by him, by an arbitrator appointed by the Mixed Arbitral Tribunal provided for in Section VI. They may be charged in the second place with payment of the amounts due in respect of claims by the nationals of such Allied or Associated Power with regard to their property, rights and interests in the territory of other enemy Powers, in so far as those claims are otherwise unsatisfied.

5.

Provides protection for an Allied Corporation from unfair use of its devices in a neutral country, through seizure of the

Notwithstanding the provisions of Article 297, where immediately before the outbreak of war a company incorporated in an Allied or Associated State had rights in common with a company controlled by it

Very special case. U. S. probably not concerned.

subsidiary of such Allied Corporation in Germany.

and incorporated in Germany to the use of trade-marks in third countries, or enjoyed the use in common with such company of unique means of reproduction of goods or articles for sale in third countries, the former company shall alone have the right to use these trade-marks in third countries to the exclusion of the German company, and these unique means of reproduction shall be handed over to the former company, notwithstanding any action taken under German war legislation with regard to the latter company or its business, industrial property or shares. Nevertheless, the former company, if requested, shall deliver the latter company derivative copies permitting the continuation of reproduction of articles for use within German territory.

6.

Up to the time when restitution is carried out in accordance with Article 297, Germany is responsible for the conservation of property, rights and interests of the nationals of Allied or Associated Powers, including companies and associations in which they are interested, that have been subjected by her to exceptional war measures.

7.

Within one year from the coming into force of the present Treaty the Allied or Associated Powers will specify the property, rights and interests over which they intend to exercise the rights provided in Article 297, paragraph (*f*).

8.

The restitution provided in Article 297 will be carried out by order of the German Government or of the authorities which have been substituted for it. Detailed accounts of the action of administrators shall be furnished to the interested persons by the German authorities upon request, which may be made at any time after the coming into force of the present Treaty.

9.

Until completion of the liquidation provided for by Article 297, paragraph (*b*), the property, rights and interests of German nationals will continue to be subject to exceptional war measures that have been or will be taken with regard to them.

Of little effect in U. S., without additional Act of Congress.

10.

Germany will, within six months from the coming into force of the present Treaty, deliver to each Allied or Associated Power all securities, certificates, deeds, or other documents of title held by its nationals and relating to property, rights or interests situated in the territory of that Allied or As-

Important clause, as we cannot adjust serious complications regarding German properties in U. S. without information sent from Germany.

sociated Power, including any shares, stock, debentures, debenture stock, or other obligations of any company incorporated in accordance with the laws of that Power.

Germany will at any time on demand of any Allied or Associated Power furnish such information as may be required with regard to the property, rights and interests of German nationals within the territory of such Allied or Associated Power, or with regard to any transactions concerning such property, rights or interests effected since July 1, 1914.

11.

The expression "cash assets" includes all deposits or funds established before or after the declaration of war, as well as all assets coming from deposits, revenues, or profits collected by administrators, sequestrators, or others from funds placed on deposit or otherwise, but does not include sums belonging to the Allied or Associated Powers or to their component States, Provinces, or Municipalities.

12.

Applies to all countries and requires funds invested to be accounted for irrespective of investment.

All investments wheresoever effected with the cash assets of nationals of the High Contracting Parties, including companies and associations in which such nationals were interested, by persons responsible for the administration of enemy properties or having control over such administration, or by order of such persons or of any authority whatsoever shall be annulled. These cash assets shall be accounted for irrespective of any such investment.

13.

Details regarding return of Allied property by Germany.

Within one month from the coming into force of the present Treaty, or on demand at any time, Germany will deliver to the Allied and Associated Powers all accounts, vouchers, records, documents and information of any kind which may be within German territory, and which concern the property, rights and interests of the nationals of those Powers, including companies and associations in which they are interested, that have been subjected to an exceptional war measure, or to a measure of transfer either in German territory or in territory occupied by Germany or her allies.

The controllers, supervisors, managers, administrators, sequestrators, liquidators and receivers shall be personally responsible under guarantee of the German Government for the immediate delivery in full of these accounts and documents, and for their accuracy.

14.

Makes clear that debts and accounts

In U. S., Alien Property Custo-

The provisions of Article 297 and this Annex relating to property, rights and in-are included as property.

terests in an enemy country, and the proceeds of the liquidation thereof, apply to debts, credits and accounts, Section III regulating only the method of payment.

dian has already adopted this method.

In the settlement of matters provided for in Article 297 between Germany and the Allied or Associated States, their colonies or protectorates, or any one of the British Dominions or India, in respect of any of which a declaration shall not have been made that they adopt Section III, and between their respective nationals, the provisions of Section III respecting the currency in which payment is to be made and the rate of exchange and of interest shall apply unless the Government of the Allied or Associated Power concerned shall within six months of the coming into force of the present Treaty notify Germany that the said provisions are not to be applied.

15.

The provisions of Article 297 and this Annex apply to industrial, literary and artistic property which has been or will be dealt with in the liquidation of property, rights, interests, companies or businesses under war legislation by the Allied or Associated Powers, or in accordance with the stipulations of Article 297, paragraph (*b*).

Section V.

CONTRACTS, PRESCRIPTIONS, JUDGMENTS.

Article 299.

General dissolution of all pre-war contracts, with certain exceptions.

Art. 299 does not apply to U. S. (See paragraph (*c*).)

(*a*) Any contracts concluded between enemies shall be regarded as having been dissolved as from the time when any two of the parties became enemies, except in respect of any debt or other pecuniary obligation arising out of any act done or money paid thereunder, and subject to the exceptions and special rules with regard to particular contracts or classes of contracts contained herein or in the Annex hereto.

(*b*) Any contract of which the execution shall be required in the general interest, within six months from the date of the coming into force of the present Treaty, by the Allied or Associated Governments of which one of the parties is a national, shall be excepted from dissolution under this Article.

When the execution of the contract thus kept alive would, owing to the alteration of trade conditions, cause one of the parties substantial prejudice the Mixed Arbitral Tribunal provided for by Section VI shall be empowered to grant to the prejudiced party equitable compensation.

(*c*) Having regard to the provisions of the constitution and law of the United States of America, of Brazil, and of Japan, neither the present Article, nor Article 300, nor the Annex hereto shall apply to contracts made between nationals of these States and German nationals; nor shall Article 305 apply to the United States of America or its nationals.

(*d*) The present Article and the Annex hereto shall not apply to contracts the parties to which became enemies by reason of one of them being an inhabitant of territory of which the sovereignty has been transferred, if such party shall acquire under the present Treaty the nationality of an Allied or Associated Power, nor shall they apply to contracts between nationals of the Allied and Associated Powers between whom trading has been prohibited by reason of one of the parties being in Allied or Associated territory in the occupation of the enemy.

(*e*) Nothing in the present Article or the Annex hereto shall be deemed to invalidate a transaction lawfully carried out in accordance with a contract between enemies if it has been carried out with the authority of one of the belligerent Powers.

ARTICLE 300.

Details with respect to Art. 299.

Art. 300 does not apply to U. S. (See Article 299(*c*).)

(*a*) All periods of prescription, or limitation of right of action, whether they began to run before or after the outbreak of war, shall be treated in the territory of the High Contracting Parties, so far as regards relations between enemies, as having been suspended for the duration of the war. They shall begin to run again at earliest three months after the coming into force of the present Treaty. This provision shall apply to the period prescribed for the presentation of interest or dividend coupons or for the presentation for repayment of securities drawn for repayment or repayable on any other ground.

(*b*) Where, on account of failure to perform any act or comply with any formality during the war, measures of execution have been taken in German territory to the prejudice of a national of an Allied or Associated Power, the claim of such national shall, if the matter does not fall within the competence of the Courts of an Allied or Associated Power, be heard by the Mixed Arbitral Tribunal provided for by Section VI.

(*c*) Upon the application of any interested person who is a national of an Allied or Associated Power the Mixed Arbitral Tribunal shall order the restoration of the rights which have been prejudiced by the measures of execution referred to in paragraph (*b*), wherever, having regard to the particular circumstances of the case, such restoration is equitable and possible.

If such restoration is inequitable or impossible the Mixed Arbitral Tribunal may grant compensation to the prejudiced party to be paid by the German Government.

(*d*) Where a contract between enemies has been dissolved by reason either of failure on the part of either party to carry out its provisions or of the exercise of a right stipulated in the contract itself the party prejudiced may apply to the Mixed Arbitral Tribunal for relief. The Tribunal will have the powers provided for in paragraph (*c*).

(*e*) The provisions of the preceding paragraphs of this Article shall apply to the nationals of Allied and Associated Powers who have been prejudiced by reason of measures referred to above taken by Germany in invaded or occupied territory, if they have not been otherwise compensated.

(*f*) Germany shall compensate any third party who may be prejudiced by any restitution or restoration ordered by the Mixed Arbitral Tribunal under the provisions of the preceding paragraphs of this Article.

(*g*) As regards negotiable instruments, the period of three months provided under paragraph (*a*) shall commence as from the date on which any exceptional regulations applied in the territories of the interested Power with regard to negotiable instruments shall have definitely ceased to have force.

Article 301.

Negotiable instruments not rendered invalid for failure to present them during the War.

Applies to U. S.

As between enemies no negotiable instrument made before the war shall be deemed to have become invalid by reason only of failure within the required time to present the instrument for acceptance or payment or to give notice of non-acceptance or non-payment to drawers or indorsers or to protest the instrument, nor by reason of failure to complete any formality during the war.

Extension of time provided for presentation, &c.

Where the period within which a negotiable instrument should have been presented for acceptance or for payment, or within which notice of non-acceptance or non-payment should have been given to the drawer or indorser, or within which the instrument should have been protested, has elapsed during the war, and the party who should have presented or protested the instrument or have given notice of non-acceptance or non-payment has failed to do so during the war, a period of not less than three months from the coming into force of the present Treaty shall be allowed within which presentation, notice of non-acceptance or non-payment or protest may be made.

ARTICLE 302.

Judgments of Courts of Allies in cases provided for in this Treaty shall be recognized as final.

Applies to U. S.

Judgments given by the Courts of an Allied or Associated Power in all cases which, under the present Treaty, they are competent to decide, shall be recognised in Germany as final, and shall be enforced without it being necessary to have them declared executory.

Remedy against judgments in German Courts when Allied defendant was not able to make defense. Function of Mixed Arbitral Tribunal of Sec. VI in such case.

If a judgment in respect to any dispute which may have arisen has been given during the war by a German Court against a national of an Allied or Associated State in a case in which he was not able to make his defence, the Allied and Associated national who has suffered prejudice thereby shall be entitled to recover compensation, to be fixed by the Mixed Arbitral Tribunal provided for in Section VI.

At the instance of the national of the Allied or Associated Power the compensation above mentioned may, upon order to that effect of the Mixed Arbitral Tribunal, be effected where it is possible by replacing the parties in the situation which they occupied before the judgment was given by the German Court.

The above compensation may likewise be obtained before the Mixed Arbitral Tribunal by the nationals of Allied or Associated Powers who have suffered prejudice by judicial measures taken in invaded or occupied territories, if they have not been otherwise compensated.

ARTICLE 303.

Meaning of "during the war."

For the purpose of Sections III, IV, V and VII, the expression "during the war" means for each Allied or Associated Power the period between the commencement of the state of war between that Power and Germany and the coming into force of the present Treaty.

ANNEX.

I. *General Provisions.*

1.

Details regarding contracts annulled by this treaty.

Does not apply to U. S.

Within the meaning of Articles 299, 300 and 301, the parties to a contract shall be regarded as enemies when trading between them shall have been prohibited by or otherwise become unlawful under laws, orders or regulations to which one of those parties was subject. They shall be deemed to have become enemies from the date when such trading was prohibited or otherwise became unlawful.

2.

The following classes of contracts are excepted from dissolution by Article 299, and, without prejudice to the rights contained in Article 297 (*b*) of Section IV, remain in force subject to the application of domestic laws, orders or regulations made during the war by the Allied and Associated Powers and subject to the terms of the contracts:

Does not apply to U. S.

(*a*) Contracts having for their object the transfer of estates or of real or personal property where the property therein had passed or the object had been delivered before the parties became enemies;

(*b*) Leases and agreements for leases of land and houses;

(*c*) Contracts of mortgage, pledge or lien;

(*d*) Concessions concerning mines, quarries or deposits;

(*e*) Contracts between individuals or companies and States, provinces, municipalities, or other similar juridical persons charged with administrative functions, and concessions granted by States, provinces, municipalities, or other similar juridical persons charged with administrative functions.

3.

If the provisions of a contract are in part dissolved under Article 299, the remaining provisions of that contract shall, subject to the same application of domestic laws as is provided for in paragraph 2, continue in force if they are severable, but where they are not severable the contract shall be deemed to have been dissolved in its entirety.

Does not apply to U. S.

II. *Provisions relating to certain classes of Contracts.*

Stock Exchange and Commercial Exchange Contracts.

Does not apply to U. S.

4.

(*a*) Rules made during the war by any recognised Exchange or Commercial Association providing for the closure of contracts entered into before the war by an enemy are confirmed by the High Contracting Parties, as also any action taken thereunder, provided:

(1) That the contract was expressed to be made subject to the rules of the Exchange or Association in question;

(2) That the rules applied to all persons concerned;

(3) That the conditions attaching to the closure were fair and reasonable.

(*b*) The preceding paragraph shall not apply to rules made during the occupation by Exchanges or Commercial Associations in the districts occupied by the enemy.

(*c*) The closure of contracts relating to cotton "futures," which were closed as on July 31, 1914, under the decision of the Liverpool Cotton Association, is also confirmed.

Security.

5.

The sale of a security held for an unpaid debt owing by an enemy shall be deemed to have been valid irrespective of notice to the owner if the creditor acted in good faith and with reasonable care and prudence, and no claim by the debtor on the ground of such sale shall be admitted.

Does not apply to U. S.

This stipulation shall not apply to any sale of securities effected by an enemy during the occupation in regions invaded or occupied by the enemy.

Negotiable Instruments.

6.

As regards Powers which adopt Section III and the Annex thereto the pecuniary

Does not apply to U. S.

obligations existing between enemies and resulting from the issue of negotiable instruments shall be adjusted in conformity with the said Annex by the instrumentality of the Clearing Offices, which shall assume the rights of the holder as regards the various remedies open to him.

7.

If a person has either before or during the war become liable upon a negotiable instrument in accordance with an undertaking given to him by a person who has subsequently become an enemy, the latter shall remain liable to indemnify the former in respect of his liability notwithstanding the outbreak of war.

Does not apply to U. S.

III. *Contracts of Insurance.*

8.

Contracts of insurance entered into by any person with another person who subsequently became an enemy will be dealt with in accordance with the following paragraphs.

Does not apply to U. S.

Fire Insurance.

9.

Contracts for the insurance of property against fire entered into by a person inter-

Does not apply to U. S.

ested in such property with another person who subsequently became an enemy shall not be deemed to have been dissolved by the outbreak of war, or by the fact of the person becoming an enemy, or on account of the failure during the war and for a period of three months thereafter to perform his obligations under the contract, but they shall be dissolved at the date when the annual premium becomes payable for the first time after the expiration of a period of three months after the coming into force of the present Treaty.

A settlement shall be effected of unpaid premiums which became due during the war, or of claims for losses which occurred during the war.

10.

Does not apply to U. S.

Where by administrative or legislative action an insurance against fire effected before the war has been transferred during the war from the original to another insurer, the transfer will be recognised and the liability of the original insurer will be deemed to have ceased as from the date of the transfer. The original insurer will, however, be entitled to receive on demand full information as to the terms of the transfer, and if it should appear that these terms were not equitable they shall be amended so far as may be necessary to render them equitable.

Furthermore, the insured shall, subject to the concurrence of the original insurer, be entitled to retransfer the contract to the original insurer as from the date of the demand.

Life Insurance.

11.

Contracts of life insurance entered into between an insurer and a person who subsequently became an enemy shall not be deemed to have been dissolved by the outbreak of war, or by the fact of the person becoming an enemy.

Does not apply to U. S.

Any sum which during the war became due upon a contract deemed not to have been dissolved under the preceding provision shall be recoverable after the war with the addition of interest at five per cent. per annum from the date of its becoming due up to the day of payment.

Where the contract has lapsed during the war owing to non-payment of premiums, or has become void from breach of the conditions of the contract, the assured or his representatives or the person entitled shall have the right at any time within twelve months of the coming into force of the present Treaty to claim from the insurer the surrender value of the policy at the date of its lapse or avoidance.

Where the contract has lapsed during the war owing to non-payment of premiums the payment of which has been prevented by the enforcement of measures of war, the assured or his representative or the persons entitled shall have the right to restore the contract on payment of the premiums with interest at five per cent. per annum within three months from the coming into force of the present Treaty.

12.

Does not apply to U. S.

Any Allied or Associated Power may within three months of the coming into force of the present Treaty cancel all the contracts of insurance running between a German insurance company and its nationals under conditions which shall protect its nationals from any prejudice.

To this end the German insurance company will hand over to the Allied or Associated Government concerned the proportion of its assets attributable to the policies so cancelled and will be relieved from all liability in respect of such policies. The assets to be handed over shall be determined by an actuary appointed by the Mixed Arbitral Tribunal.

13.

Where contracts of life insurance have been entered into by a local branch of an insurance company established in a country which subsequently became an enemy country, the contract shall, in the absence of any stipulation to the contrary in the contract itself, be governed by the local law, but the insurer shall be entitled to demand from the insured or his representatives the refund of sums paid on claims made or enforced under measures taken during the war, if the making or enforcement of such claims was not in accordance with the terms of the contract itself or was not consistent with the laws or treaties existing at the time when it was entered into.

Does not apply to U. S.

14.

In any case where by the law applicable to the contract the insurer remains bound by the contract notwithstanding the non-payment of premiums until notice is given to the insured of the termination of the contract, he shall be entitled where the giving of such notice was prevented by the war to recover the unpaid premiums with interest at five per cent. per annum from the insured.

Does not apply to U. S.

15.

Insurance contracts shall be considered as contracts of life assurance for the pur-

Does not apply to U. S.

pose of paragraphs 11 to 14 when they depend on the probabilities of human life combined with the rate of interest for the calculation of the reciprocal engagements between the two parties.

Marine Insurance.

16.

Contracts of marine insurance including time policies and voyage policies entered into between an insurer and a person who subsequently became an enemy, shall be deemed to have been dissolved on his becoming an enemy, except in cases where the risk undertaken in the contract had attached before he became an enemy.

Does not apply to U. S.

Where the risk had not attached, money paid by way of premium or otherwise shall be recoverable from the insurer.

Where the risk had attached effect shall be given to the contract notwithstanding the party becoming an enemy, and sums due under the contract either by way of premiums or in respect of losses shall be recoverable after the coming into force of the present Treaty.

In the event of any agreement being come to for the payment of interest on sums due before the war to or by the nationals of States which have been at war and recovered after the war, such interest shall in the case of losses recoverable under contracts of marine insurance run from the expiration of a period of one year from the date of the loss.

17.

No contract of marine insurance with an insured person who subsequently became an enemy shall be deemed to cover losses due to belligerent action by the Power of which the insurer was a national or by the allies or associates of such Power.

Does not apply to U. S.

18.

Where it is shown that a person who had before the war entered into a contract of marine insurance with an insurer who subsequently became an enemy entered after the outbreak of war into a new contract covering the same risk with an insurer who was not an enemy, the new contract shall be deemed to be substituted for the original contract as from the date when it was entered into, and the premiums payable shall be adjusted on the basis of the original insurer having remained liable on the contract only up till the time when the new contract was entered into.

Does not apply to U. S.

Other Insurances.

19.

Contracts of insurance entered into before the war between an insurer and a person who subsequently became an enemy, other than contracts dealt with in paragraphs 9 to 18, shall be treated in all respects on the same footing as contracts of fire insurance between the same persons would be dealt with under the said paragraphs.

Does not apply to U.S.

Re-insurance.

20.

All treaties of re-insurance with a person who became an enemy shall be regarded as having been abrogated by the person becoming an enemy, but without prejudice in the case of life or marine risks which had attached before the war to the right to recover payment after the war for sums due in respect of such risks.

Does not apply to U. S.

Nevertheless if, owing to invasion, it has been impossible for the re-insured to find another re-insurer, the treaty shall remain in force until three months after the coming into force of the present Treaty.

Where a re-insurance treaty becomes void under this paragraph, there shall be an adjustment of accounts between the parties in respect both of premiums paid and payable and of liabilities for losses in respect of life or marine risks which had attached before the war. In the case of risks other than those mentioned in paragraphs 11 to 18 the adjustment of accounts shall be made as at the date of the parties becoming enemies without regard to claims for losses which may have occurred since that date.

21.

The provisions of the preceding paragraph will extend equally to re-insurances existing at the date of the parties becoming enemies of particular risks undertaken by the insurer in a contract of insurance against any risks other than life or marine risks.

Does not apply to U. S.

22.

Re-insurance of life risks effected by particular contracts and not under any general treaty remain in force.

Does not apply to U. S.

The provisions of paragraph 12 apply to treaties of re-insurance of life insurance contracts in which enemy companies are the re-insurers.

23.

In case of a re-insurance effected before the war of a contract of marine insurance,

Does not apply to U. S.

the cession of a risk which had been ceded to the re-insurer shall, if it had attached before the outbreak of war, remain valid and effect be given to the contract notwithstanding the outbreak of war; sums due under the contract of re-insurance in respect either of premiums or of losses shall be recoverable after the war.

24.

Does not apply to U. S.

The provisions of paragraphs 17 and 18 and the last part of paragraph 16 shall apply to contracts for the re-insurance of marine risks.

SECTION VI.

MIXED ARBITRAL TRIBUNAL.

ARTICLE 304.

Creation of Mixed Arbitral Tribunal between each allied state and Germany.

Applies to U. S.

(*a*) Within three months from the date of the coming into force of the present Treaty, a Mixed Arbitral Tribunal shall be established between each of the Allied and Associated Powers on the one hand and Germany on the other hand. Each such Tribunal shall consist of three members. Each of the Governments concerned shall appoint one of these members. The President shall be chosen by agreement between the two Governments concerned.

In case of failure to reach agreement, the President of the Tribunal and two other persons either of whom may in case of need take his place, shall be chosen by the Council of the League of Nations, or, until this is set up, by M. Gustave Ador if he is willing. These persons shall be nationals of Powers that have remained neutral during the war.

M. Ador is the present (1919) president of the Swiss Republic.

If any Government does not proceed within a period of one month in case there is a vacancy to appoint a member of the Tribunal, such member shall be chosen by the other Government from the two persons mentioned above other than the President.

The decision of the majority of the members of the Tribunal shall be the decision of the Tribunal.

Jurisdiction of Mixed Arbitral Tribunals.

(*b*) The Mixed Arbitral Tribunals established pursuant to paragraph (*a*), shall decide all questions within their competence under Sections III, IV, V and VII.

In addition, all questions, whatsoever their nature, relating to contracts concluded before the coming into force of the present Treaty between nationals of the Allied and Associated Powers and German nationals shall be decided by the Mixed Arbitral Tribunal, always excepting questions which, under the laws of the Allied, Associated or Neutral Powers, are within the jurisdiction of the National

Courts of those Powers. Such questions shall be decided by the National Courts in question, to the exclusion of the Mixed Arbitral Tribunal. The party who is a national of an Allied or Associated Power may nevertheless bring the case before the Mixed Arbitral Tribunal if this is not prohibited by the laws of his country.

(*c*) If the number of cases justifies it, additional members shall be appointed and each Mixed Arbitral Tribunal shall sit in divisions. Each of these divisions will be constituted as above.

(*d*) Each Mixed Arbitral Tribunal will settle its own procedure except in so far as it is provided in the following Annex, and is empowered to award the sums to be paid by the loser in respect of the costs and expenses of the proceedings.

(*e*) Each Government will pay the remuneration of the member of the Mixed Arbitral Tribunal appointed by it and of any agent whom it may appoint to represent it before the Tribunal. The remuneration of the President will be determined by special agreement between the Governments concerned; and this remuneration and the joint expenses of each Tribunal will be paid by the two Governments in equal moieties.

(*f*) The High Contracting Parties agree that their courts and authorities shall render to the Mixed Arbitral Tribunals direct all the assistance in their power, particularly as regards transmitting notices and collecting evidence.

(*g*) The High Contracting Parties agree to regard the decisions of the Mixed Arbitral Tribunal as final and conclusive, and to render them binding upon their nationals.

ANNEX.

1.

Should one of the members of the Tribunal either die, retire, or be unable for any reason whatever to discharge his function, the same procedure will be followed for filling the vacancy as was followed for appointing him.

2.

The Tribunal may adopt such rules of procedure as shall be in accordance with justice and equity and decide the order and time at which each party must conclude its arguments, and may arrange all formalities required for dealing with the evidence.

3.

The agent and counsel of the parties on each side are authorised to present orally and in writing to the Tribunal arguments in support or in defence of each case.

4.

The Tribunal shall keep record of the questions and cases submitted and the proceedings thereon, with the dates of such proceedings.

5.

Each of the Powers concerned may appoint a secretary. These secretaries shall act together as joint secretaries of the Tribunal and shall be subject to its direction. The Tribunal may appoint and employ any other necessary officer or officers to assist in the performance of its duties.

6.

The Tribunal shall decide all questions and matters submitted upon such evidence and information as may be furnished by the parties concerned.

7.

Germany agrees to give the Tribunal all facilities and information required by it for carrying out its investigations.

8.

The language in which the proceedings shall be conducted shall, unless otherwise agreed, be English, French, Italian or Japanese, as may be determined by the Allied or Associated Power concerned.

9.

The place and time for the meetings of each Tribunal shall be determined by the President of the Tribunal.

ARTICLE 305.

Does not apply to U. S. (See Article 299(c).)

Whenever a competent court has given or gives a decision in a case covered by Sections III, IV, V or VII, and such decision is inconsistent with the provisions of such Sections, the party who is prejudiced by the decision shall be entitled to obtain redress which shall be fixed by the Mixed Arbitral Tribunal. At the request of the national of an Allied or Associated Power, the redress may, whenever possible, be effected by the Mixed Arbitral Tribunal directing the replacement of the parties in the position occupied by them before the judgment was given by the German court.

SECTION VII.

INDUSTRIAL PROPERTY.

ARTICLE 306.

Re-establishes industrial property rights in

Restoration is subject to limitations of the following clauses.

Subject to the stipulations of the present Treaty, rights of industrial, literary and ar-

favor of persons entitled thereto when War commenced.

tistic property, as such property is defined by the International Conventions of Paris and of Berne, mentioned in Article 286, shall be re-established or restored, as from the coming into force of the present Treaty, in the territories of the High Contracting Parties, in favour of the persons entitled to the benefit of them at the moment when the state of war commenced or their legal representatives. Equally, rights which, except for the war, would have been acquired during the war in consequence of an application made for the protection of industrial property, or the publication of a literary or artistic work, shall be recognised and established in favour of those persons who would have been entitled thereto, from the coming into force of the present Treaty.

Provides for recognition of rights which, except for the War, would have been acquired, in consequence of an application for protection of industrial property.

Acts of Allies under special War Measures to remain valid and effective.

Nevertheless, all acts done by virtue of the special measures taken during the war under legislative, executive or administrative authority of any Allied or Associated Power in regard to the rights of German nationals in industrial, literary or artistic property shall remain in force and shall continue to maintain their full effect.

Allied Governments and persons acting on their behalf absolved from claims for use of German Industrial Property during the

No claim shall be made or action brought by Germany or German nationals in respect of the use during the war by the Government of any Allied or Associated Power, or by any persons acting on behalf or with

War; also from claims for sale and use thereafter of resulting products.

the assent of such Government, of any rights in industrial, literary or artistic property, nor in respect of the sale, offering for sale, or use of any products, articles or apparatus whatsoever to which such rights applied.

Sums due or paid under Special War Measures of Allies to be treated in same manner as other sums due to German nationals. Sums produced by Special War Measures of Germany to be treated in same way as other debts of German nationals.

Unless the legislation of any one of the Allied or Associated Powers in force at the moment of the signature of the present Treaty otherwise directs, sums due or paid in virtue of any act or operation resulting from the execution of the special measures mentioned in paragraph I of this Article shall be dealt with in the same way as other sums due to German nationals are directed to be dealt with by the present Treaty; and sums produced by any special measures taken by the German Government in respect of rights in industrial, literary or artistic property belonging to the nationals of the Allied or Associated Powers shall be considered and treated in the same way as other debts due from German nationals.

Allies reserve right after War to impose restrictions on German Industrial Property in public interest, or for national defense.

Each of the Allied and Associated Powers reserves to itself the right to impose such limitations, conditions or restrictions on rights of industrial, literary or artistic property (with the exception of trade-marks) acquired before or during the war, or which may be subsequently acquired in accordance with its legislation, by German nationals, whether by granting licenses, or by the working, or by preserving control over their exploitation, or in any other way, as may be considered necessary for national defence, or in the public interest, or for assuring the fair treatment by Germany of the rights of industrial, literary and artistic property held in German territory by its nationals, or for securing the due fulfilment of all the obligations undertaken by Germany in the present Treaty. As regards rights of industrial, literary and artistic property acquired after the coming into force of the present Treaty, the right so reserved by the Allied and Associated Powers shall only be exercised in cases where these limitations, conditions or restrictions may be considered necessary for national defence or in the public interest.

In the event of such restriction, reasonable indemnities will be paid.

In the event of the application of the provisions of the preceding paragraph by any Allied or Associated Power, there shall be paid reasonable indemnities or royalties, which shall be dealt with in the same way as other sums due to German nationals are directed to be dealt with by the present Treaty.

Transfers during the War or thereafter may be treated by Allies as void if they would result in defeating objects of this Article.

Necessary to prevent fraudulent transfers to neutrals.

Each of the Allied or Associated Powers reserves the right to treat as void and of no effect any transfer in whole or in part of or other dealing with rights of or in respect of industrial, literary or artistic property effected after August 1, 1914, or in the future, which would have the result of defeating the objects of the provisions of this Article.

Industrial property which has been or may be dealt with under War legislation by Allies in liquidation of business not subject to provisions of this Article.

The provisions of this Article shall not apply to rights in industrial, literary or artistic property which have been dealt with in the liquidation of business or companies under war legislation by the Allied or Associated Powers, or which may be so dealt with by virtue of Article 297, paragraph (*b*).

ARTICLE 307.

Extension of one year provided within which to satisfy any obligation provided by laws or regulations relating to industrial property acquired before Aug. 1, 1914, or which might have been acquired during the War from an application made before or during the War.

Applies to all signatories inter se, but excepts U. S. interference proceedings.

A minimum of one year after the coming into force of the present Treaty shall be accorded to the nationals of the High Contracting Parties, without extension fees or other penalty, in order to enable such persons to accomplish any act, fulfil any formality, pay any fees, and generally satisfy any obligation prescribed by the laws or regulations of the respective States relating to the obtaining, preserving, or opposing rights to, or in respect of, industrial property either acquired before August 1, 1914, or which, except for the war, might have been acquired since that date as a result of an application made before the war or during its continuance, but nothing in this Article shall give any right to reopen interference proceedings in the United States of

America where a final hearing has taken place.

All lapsed industrial property rights revived; subject, in the case of patents and designs to imposition of conditions by Allies to protect intervening manufacture and use.

Where German patent rights revive they are subject to same license provisions applicable during the War, and to all the provisions of this Treaty.

All rights in, or in respect of, such property which may have lapsed by reason of any failure to accomplish any act, fulfil any formality, or make any payment, shall revive, but subject in the case of patents and designs to the imposition of such conditions as each Allied or Associated Power may deem reasonably necessary for the protection of persons who have manufactured or made use of the subject matter of such property while the rights had lapsed. Further, where rights to patents or designs belonging to German nationals are revived under this Article, they shall be subject in respect of the grant of licenses to the same provisions as would have been applicable to them during the war, as well as to all the provisions of the present Treaty.

No rights lost for failure to exploit during the War, nor for two years thereafter.

Applies equally to all countries.

The period from August 1, 1914, until the coming into force of the present Treaty shall be excluded in considering the time within which a patent should be worked or a trade-mark or design used, and it is further agreed that no patent, registered trade-mark or design in force on August 1, 1914, shall be subject to revocation or cancellation by reason only of the failure to work such patent or use such trade-mark or design for two years after the coming into force of the present Treaty.

Article 308.

Priority rights of the International Convention extended during War and six months after.

Applies to all signatories inter se.

The rights of priority, provided by Article 4 of the International Convention for the Protection of Industrial Property of Paris, of March 20, 1883, revised at Washington in 1911 or by any other Convention or Statute, for the filing or registration of applications for patents or models of utility, and for the registration of trade-marks, designs and models which had not expired on August 1, 1914, and those which have arisen during the war, or would have arisen but for the war, shall be extended by each of the High Contracting Parties in favour of all nationals of the other High Contracting Parties for a period of six months after the coming into force of the present Treaty.

Protection of all bona fide third persons having intervening rights.

Nevertheless, such extension shall in no way affect the right of any of the High Contracting Parties or of any person who before the coming into force of the present Treaty was *bona fide* in possession of any rights of industrial property conflicting with rights applied for by another who claims rights of priority in respect of them, to exercise such rights by itself or himself personally, or by such agents or licensees as derived their rights from it or him before the coming into force of the present Treaty; and such persons shall not be amenable to any action or other process of law in respect of infringement.

ARTICLE 309.

Cancels all rights to sue for infringements committed during the War.

This article does not apply to U. S. (See closing paragraph.)

No action shall be brought and no claim made by persons residing or carrying on business within the territories of Germany on the one part and of the Allied or Associated Powers on the other, or persons who are nationals of such Powers respectively, or by any one deriving title during the war from such persons, by reason of any action which has taken place within the territory of the other party between the date of the declaration of war and that of the coming into force of the present Treaty, which might constitute an infringement of the rights of industrial property or rights of literary and artistic property, either existing at any time during the war or revived under the provisions of Articles 307 and 308.

Immunity as to sales of infringing articles extended one year after the War.

Equally, no action for infringement of industrial, literary or artistic property rights by such persons shall at any time be permissible in respect of the sale or offering for sale for a period of one year after the signature of the present Treaty in the territories of the Allied or Associated Powers on the one hand or Germany on the other, of products or articles manufactured, or of literary or artistic works published, during the period between the declaration of war and the signature of the present Treaty, or against those who have acquired and continue to use them. It is understood, nevertheless, that this provision shall not apply when the possessor of the rights was domiciled or had an industrial or commercial establishment in the districts occupied by Germany during the war.

Provision does not apply when possessor of rights was domiciled or in business in districts occupied by Germany during the War.

This Article shall not apply as between the United States of America on the one hand and Germany on the other.

ARTICLE 310.

Cancels all pre-War licenses. Licenses may be renewed on conditions fixed by tribunal of country where the rights licensed originated; except when rights originated in Germany, in which case Mixed Arbitral Tribunal fixes renewal conditions.

This article does not apply to U. S. at all. (See closing paragraph.)

Licenses in respect of industrial, literary or artistic property concluded before the war between nationals of the Allied or Associated Powers or persons residing in their territory or carrying on business therein, on the one part, and German nationals, on the other part, shall be considered as cancelled as from the date of the declaration of war between Germany and the Allied or Associated Powers. But, in any case, the former beneficiary of a contract of this kind shall have the right, within a period of six months after the coming into force of the present Treaty, to demand from the proprietor of the rights the grant of a new license, the conditions of which, in default of agreement between the parties, shall be fixed by the duly qualified tribunal in the country under whose legislation the rights had been acquired, except in the case of licenses held in respect of rights acquired under German law. In such cases the conditions shall be fixed by the Mixed Arbitral Tribunal referred to in Section VI of this Part. The tribunal may, if necessary, fix also the amount which it may deem just should be paid by reason of the use of the rights during the war.

Tribunal may also fix amount payable for use of rights during the War.

No license granted by an Allied Government during the War shall be affected by a pre-War license.

No license in respect of industrial, literary or artistic property, granted under the special war legislation of any Allied or Associated Power, shall be affected by the continued existence of any license entered into before the war, but shall remain valid and of full effect, and a license so granted to the former beneficiary of a license entered into before the war shall be considered as substituted for such license.

Royalties paid on pre-War licenses during the War shall be dealt with in the same manner as other debts or credits of German nationals.

Where sums have been paid during the war by virtue of a license or agreement concluded before the war in respect of rights of industrial property or for the reproduction or the representation of literary, dramatic or artistic works, these sums shall be dealt with in the same manner as other debts or credits of German nationals, as provided by the present Treaty.

This Article shall not apply as between the United States of America on the one hand and Germany on the other.

ARTICLE 311.

German industrial property rights owned by inhabitants of territory separated from Germany to remain valid in Germany.

The inhabitants of territories separated from Germany by virtue of the present Treaty shall, notwithstanding this separation and the change of nationality consequent thereon, continue to enjoy in Germany all the rights in industrial, literary and artistic property to which they were entitled under German legislation at the time of the separation.

Such industrial property rights shall also be recognized by and remain in force in the State to which the territory is transferred.

Rights of industrial, literary and artistic property which are in force in the territories separated from Germany under the present Treaty at the moment of the separation of these territories from Germany, or which will be re-established or restored in accordance with the provisions of Article 306 of the present Treaty, shall be recognised by the State to which the said territory is transferred and shall remain in force in that territory for the same period of time given them under the German law.

[NOTE—The following articles were among the Economic Clauses originally drafted, but they were transferred.]

PORTS, WATERWAYS AND RAILWAYS.

SECTION I.

GENERAL PROVISIONS.

ARTICLE 323.

Germany undertakes to make no discrimination or preference, direct or indirect, in the duties, charges and prohibitions relating to importations into or exportations from her territories, or, subject to the special engagements contained in the present Treaty, in the charges and conditions of transport of goods or persons entering or leaving her territories, based on the frontier crossed; or on the kind, ownership or flag of the means of transport (including aircraft) employed; or on the original or immediate place of departure of the vessel, wagon or aircraft or other means of transport employed, or its ultimate or intermediate destination; or on the route of or places of transshipment on the journey; or on whether any port through which the goods are imported or exported is a German port or a port belonging to any foreign country or on whether the goods are imported or exported by sea, by land or by air.

Germany particularly undertakes not to establish against the ports and vessels of any of the Allied and Associated Powers any surtax or any direct or indirect bounty for export or import by German ports or vessels, or by those of another Power, for example by means of combined tariffs. She further undertakes that persons or goods passing through a port or using a vessel of any of the Allied and Associated Powers shall not be subjected to any formality or delay whatever to which such persons or goods would not be subjected if they passed through a German port or a port of any other Power, or used a German vessel or a vessel of any other Power.

SECTION II.

NAVIGATION.

CHAPTER I.

FREEDOM OF NAVIGATION.

ARTICLE 327.

Shipping of Allies to have national treatment in Germany.

This privilege to endure for five years, and thereafter to be available only to such Allies as grant reciprocity; subject, however, to revision by League of Nations. (See Article 378.)

The nationals of any of the Allied and Associated Powers as well as their vessels and property shall enjoy in all German ports and on the inland navigation routes of Germany the same treatment in all respects as German nationals, vessels and property.

In particular the vessels of any one of the Allied or Associated Powers shall be entitled to transport goods of any description, and passengers, to or from any ports or places in German territory to which German vessels may have access, under conditions which shall not be more onerous than those applied in the case of national vessels; they shall be treated on a footing of equality with national vessels as regards port and harbour facilities and charges of every description, including facilities for stationing, loading and unloading, and duties and charges of tonnage, harbour, pilotage, lighthouse, quarantine, and all analogous duties and charges of whatsoever nature, levied in the name of or for the profit of the Government, public functionaries, private individuals, corporations or establishments of any kind.

In the event of Germany granting a preferential régime to any of the Allied or Associated Powers or to any other foreign Power, this régime shall be extended immediately and unconditionally to all the Allied and Associated Powers.

There shall be no impediment to the movement of persons or vessels other than those arising from prescriptions concerning customs, police, sanitation, emigration and immigration, and those relating to the import and export of prohibited goods. Such regulations must be reasonable and uniform and must not impede traffic unnecessarily.

Chapter II.

FREE ZONES IN PORTS.

Article 328.

The free zones existing in German ports on August 1, 1914, shall be maintained. These free zones, and any other free zones which may be established in German territory by the present Treaty, shall be subject to the régime provided for in the following Articles.

Goods entering or leaving a free zone shall not be subjected to any import or export duty, other than those provided for in Article 330.

Vessels and goods entering a free zone may be subjected to the charges established to cover expenses of administration, upkeep and improvement of the port, as well as to the charges for the use of various installations, provided that these charges shall be reasonable having regard to the expenditure incurred, and shall be levied in the conditions of equality provided for in Article 327.

ADDENDA

ADDENDA.

THE PRINCIPLES OF REPARATION.

Address on Behalf of the American Delegates By John Foster Dulles, Esq., on February 13, 1919.

Mr. President:

It was a matter of considerable chagrin to the American members of this commission when it developed, upon an analysis of the various memoranda on principles of reparation, that the memorandum of the United States appeared to be the least drastic in its terms. It was a matter of chagrin because a lack of severity in such an expression of principles is liable to be misconstrued as indicative of a lack of severity in judgment and in purpose. In fact, the American members associate themselves in the most complete and unconditional way with all that has been said in the various memoranda on file relative to the enormity of the crime which Germany has committed, and they adhere to the bitter denunciation of this crime which was so eloquently expressed on Monday in the powerful address of the Hon. Mr. Hughes.

And if the character of our proposals is not attributable to a lack of severity in our condemnation of Germany, no more does it indicate that the Government and people of the United States are indifferent to the war costs with which they themselves are burdened. For we too have our war debt. In magnitude it is comparable to that of any other nation, and it constitutes a fearful burden, which is absorbing, and for many years will absorb, the greater part of the nation's income, and it seriously threatens the vitality of our economic life.

If then it is in accordance with our sentiment that the principles of reparation be severe, and in accord with our material interest that these principles be all inclusive, why, in defiance of these motives, have we proposed reparation in certain limited ways only? It is because, gentlemen, we do not regard ourselves as free. We are not here to consider as a novel proposal what reparation the enemy should in justice pay; we have not before us a blank page upon which we are free to write what we will. We have before us a page, it is true; but one which is already filled with writing, and at the bottom are the signatures of Mr. Wilson, of Mr. Orlando, of Mr. Clemenceau, and of Mr. Lloyd George.

You are all aware, I am sure, of the writing to which I refer: It is the agreed basis of peace with Germany. It consists, so far as is relevant to our discussion here, of the Fourteen Points contained in an address of President Wilson of January 8, 1918, which, with certain qualifications, were accepted by the Allies, by the United States, and by Germany as the agreed basis of peace. On these terms, says the Allied memorandum, "they declare their willingness to make peace with the Government of Germany." This offer was accepted by the Government of Germany, and in reliance on the agreement resulting from such acceptance the enemy laid down his arms.

Among the terms of peace which were accepted by both sides we find provisions relative to reparation. What are these provisions?

The address of January 8th says:

> Belgium, the whole world will agree, must be evacuated and restored. * * * All French territory should be freed and the invaded portions restored. * * * Rumania, Serbia, and Montenegro should be evacuated; occupied territory restored.

The Allied qualification or enlargement of these provisions is contained in the following language:

> The President declared that invaded territories must be restored as well as evacuated and freed. The Allied Governments feel that no doubt ought to be allowed to exist as to what this provision implies. By it they understand that compensation will be made by Germany for all damage done to the civilian population of the Allies and their property by the aggression of Germany by land, by sea, and from the air.

The foregoing language thus constitutes, in so far as reparation is concerned, the terms upon which the United States and the Allies agreed to make peace with Germany and the terms upon which Germany accepted the armistice of November 11, 1918.

Gentlemen, we have here an agreement. It is an agreement which cannot be ignored, and I am confident that no one here would propose to ignore it. I know that I have the full concurrence of all in the proposition that if this agreement constitutes a limitation upon our right to demand reparation of the enemy, that limitation will be respected.

And can there be any question that this agreement does constitute a limitation?

It is perfectly obvious that it was recognized at the time of the negotiations in October and November, 1918, that the reparation then specified for would limit the Associated Governments as to the reparation which they could demand of the enemy as a condition of peace. The whole purpose of Germany was to ascertain the maximum which would be demanded of her in the terms of peace, and the action of the Allies in especially stipulating at that time for an enlargement of the original proposal respecting reparation is explicable only on the theory that it was understood that once an agreement was concluded they would no longer be free to specify the reparation which Germany must make.

We have thus agreed that we would give Germany peace if she would do certain specified things. Is it now open to us to say, "Yes; but before you get peace you must do other and further things"? We have said to Germany, "You may have peace if among other things you perform certain acts of reparation which will cost you, say, ten billion dollars." Are we not now clearly precluded from saying, "You can have peace provided you perform other acts of reparation which will bring your total liability to many times that which was originally stipulated." No; irrespective of the justice of the enemy making the latter reparation, it is now too late. Our bargain has been struck for better or for worse; it remains only to give it a fair construction and practical application.

The fundamental proposition, therefore, put forth by the American members of this commission is that we demand of Germany, as a condition of peace, all of that reparation, but only that, stipulated for by a fair construction of the agreement with Germany as to what the terms of peace should be.

This is a proposition from which, frankly, I do not see how any one of us can dissent. It is, perhaps, unnecessary for me to have pressed and emphasized this point as I have done, and I would not have done so except that I have been struck by the fact that in none of the memoranda of principles which have been filed save that of the United States and of Serbia, is there any reference to the agreement as to what should be the terms of peace. The American delegation have, therefore, felt the advisability of drawing this matter to the attention of the commission, and of proposing, as the starting point in our deliberations, the language relative to reparation contained in the agreement with Germany as to the terms upon which she could have peace.

If this proposition is sound, our task bcomes one of construction rather than of original thought. We may have, and I have no doubt that we all do have, very definite views as to the reparation which could in justice be required of Germany. But the occasion for the presentation of such original views was in the early days of November, 1918, and not today. Today we find the question prejudged, and however strongly we may feel that the reparation stipulated for at that time falls short of what the enemy ought to pay, we must accept the decision of those who then had the power of decision in their hands. Is it not fair to assume that they judged that to prolong the war for the purpose of securing a theoretical right to full reparation would have been to sacrifice substance to form, since it would have meant balancing the problematic ability of the enemy to pay against the real and vital expenditure in life and in money which every day of war entailed?

We pass then to the construction and application of the agreed terms of peace. The construction proposed by the American members is set forth rather fully in the memorandum which has been filed and a copy of which is in the hands of each of you. Briefly, we take the view that the terms of peace proposed and accepted are not to be construed as waiving any clear right of reparation due under accepted principles of international law. We thus recognize that our agreement with Germany is not in derogation of those principles of jurisprudence upon which the French memorandum and upon which Mr. Hughes' address purport to base themselves. But we are also compelled to recognize that in so far as we base our claims, not upon contractional law but on the law of torts, we are restricted to damage arising from *illegal* acts. It is not enough that an act be immoral, that it be cruel, that it be unjust, unless at the same time it be illegal. It is the quality of illegality alone which in law gives rise to a right of reparation. International law and the municipal jurisprudence of all civilized nations are in accord in this respect.

Accordingly it is the American proposition that where the enemy has committed an act clearly violative of international law as existing at the time of the commission of the act, he is liable to make reparation for the damage caused thereby. This involves the complete repayment to Belgium of the damage to her resulting from Germany's violation of her covenant not to make war upon Belgium. The illegality of this act and the duty of making reparation have already been formally admitted by Germany. It further means that the enemy is liable for damage resulting from such miscellaneous illegal acts as the deportation of civilians, attacks on undefended towns, sinkings of merchant vessels without warning, and other illegal acts too numerous to mention here.

In addition to this reparation due in accordance with recognized international law, there is the reparation which it was expressly agreed should become a part of the Treaty of Peace, and which reparation, to some extent, includes that due in accordance with international law, but which to a considerable extent goes beyond. This reparation expressly stipulated for involves a restoration of the invaded areas of Belgium, France, Rumania, Serbia, and Montenegro, and compensation for all damage done to the civilian population of the Allies and their property by the aggression of Germany by land, by sea, and from the air. The American members have given in their memorandum a statement of what reparation they believe to be due in accordance with the foregoing stipulation. The construction there given is one which we believe to be fair, but which we also recognize is open to question in some respects and can advantageously be made the subject of an interchange of ideas. I know I may safely say that nothing is further from the intention and desire of the American members than that any construction should be given those words which will save the enemy from making reparation which he can fairly be said to have agreed to when he accepted the proposition of the Associated Governments relative to the terms of peace. It is our desire to see reparation made to the uttermost limit; the limit being a fair construction of the agreed terms of peace.

I accordingly have the honor to propose, on behalf of the American members of this commission, that the commission accept as a fundamental principle that the reparation to be exacted from the enemy is that which is due in accordance with a fair construction of the written agreement of the Associated Governments with Germany as the terms of peace.

I further suggest, on behalf of the American members, that the commission next consider the most expeditious method of reaching an agreement as to the construction and application of the language of the agreement relative to reparation.

Speech by the Rt. Hon. W. M. Hughes, Prime Minister of Australia, Before the Commission on Reparation, on February 14, 1919.

The Principle.

In the memorandum filed by the British delegation to this commission, and in the speech made by me at the sitting of the commission on February 10th, it was established that the principle of reparation justified a claim by the Allies for reimbursement generally of the damage and cost to the Allies which were the natural consequence of the aggressive war launched against the Allies by the enemy Powers.

Suggested Limitation.

The memorandum filed by the American delegation, and the able addresses in support by Mr. Dulles, suggest that the right to general reparation has been to some extent limited by the acceptance by the Allies—with certain reservations—of President Wilson's Fourteen Points; though it is admitted that the right extends much beyond the particular items of reparation specified in the Points.

This raises an issue of fundamental importance. Its discussion involves further consideration of the principles, and a fuller reference to the correspondence between the Governments of the United States and of Germany prior to the armistice, than is made in the American memorandum.

I think I shall best serve the purpose we all have in view if I deal first with the points raised by Mr. Dulles and by the American memorandum regarding the effects of international law upon claims for reparation; secondly with the position alleged to have been created by the acceptance by Allies of President Wilson's terms of peace, and lastly refer very briefly to the parts of Mr. Dulles' argument especially that part which seemed to imply that reparation was a right arising out of contract between the victors and the vanquished.

1. INTERNATIONAL LAW.

First, then, as to the effect of international law upon the right of reparation.

The principle is accepted by the American delegation that, outside of the Fourteen Points and unaffected by them:

> Reparation is due for all damage directly consequent upon acts of the enemy clearly in violation of international law as recognized at the time of the commission of the acts in question.

This is an admission that goes to the very root of the whole question. It means, in the first place, that there are basic rights of reparation, which we have not by any implication bargained away. But in the statement of the principle upon which these rights are founded, the American memorandum takes a too narrow view restricting it to acts of the enemy in *violation of international law.*

Lord Sumner has already pointed out that there is no rule of international law which so limits our rights. Nor indeed is there anything in the American memorandum to establish this limitation except a mere declaration wholly unsupported by reasons. A belligerent is entitled to demand from a defeated enemy compensation for all the loss and damage due to the enemy's aggression, independently of the question whether the war waged by the enemy, or anything done by the enemy in the course of the war, was in violation of international law.

Neutralization of Belgium.

But, even taking the American proposition as it stands, let us see how far it leads us in relation to the outstanding fact of the neutralization of Belgium.

That neutralization, of course, flows from a treaty —from an agreement between certain nations. International law knows nothing of neutralization except as arising out of treaty, and therefore we are to look only to that branch of international law which deals with the observance of treaties.

Rights of Signatories.

The American memorandum admits that Belgium's whole war costs are a direct consequence of Germany's violation of Belgium's right of neutrality. That is indisputable; but we cannot stop there. The neutralization of Belgium was not an isolated fact; it was not a matter between Belgium and Germany alone. Belgium's neutrality was the result of an agreement between certain nations. It was guaranteed by all the signatory powers to the Treaty of London—among them being Great Britain and France. Great Britain and France were bound by their treaty obligation to defend Belgium's neutrality; and consequently Germany's violation of that neutrality involved, as a direct and necessary consequence, the whole war costs, not only of Belgium, but of Great Britain and France as well.

It is self-evident that if Germany's breach of international law by the invasion of Belgium involves the payment by Germany of Belgium's war costs, it equally involves the payment of the war costs of those signatories to the Treaty of London who guaranteed Belgium's neutrality.

Rights of Non-Signatories.

But more is involved than even this. The Treaty of London was much more than a contract between the signatories. It was a public international pledge relating, not to a matter which concerned the signatory parties only, but to a matter which concerned the whole world—namely, the preservation of the world's peace. The signatory parties bound themselves to guarantee the observance of the treaty; but the whole world had a right to its observance and if the need arose to assist in its enforcement. When Germany violated the treaty, Great Britain and France were *bound* to defend it;

the United States and Italy were *entitled* to defend it. Germany was the criminal, Belgium the victim. Great Britain and France may be compared to the policemen whose sworn task is to prevent a breach of the law; the United States and Italy and other nations may be compared to civilians whose right it is—and also whose duty in case of need—to come to the rescue.

Germany's violation of her international pledge was an act which the whole world had a right to resist; and it follows beyond the possibility of dispute that the whole war costs of the Associated Powers, being a direct consequence of that violation, can also be claimed, and that—even on the narrow basis of the American memorandum—reparation for all those war costs is clearly due from Germany.

Rights Independent of International Law.

But I have already said that we do not accept that narrow basis. We submit that the obligation to make reparation is not limited to cases where a breach of international law is proved. We submit that the reparation, which we are justly entitled to claim, is that reparation which the principle of justice requires to be paid—the principle that the cost of a wrong should be borne by the wrong-doer—the cost of an unjust war by the aggressors. This too, as clearly shown by Lord Sumner yesterday, is in accordance with international law.

2. The Terms and Principles of Peace.

The American delegate contended, however, that this right had been lost by the acceptance of President Wilson's Fourteen Points. Lord Sumner has already dealt with this argument effectively; but I will add some further considerations.

President Wilson's Addresses.

Examination of President Wilson's addresses, which are referred to in the correspondence between President Wilson and Germany, and between President Wilson and the Allies, shows that this principle of justice has been explicitly accepted by the Associated Powers and by Germany. Apart altogether from any rules of international law, we are able to reply on the definite principles laid down by President Wilson himself, in the correspondence referred to in the note of November 5th, and accepted by the Allies and by Germany as the basis of a peace of justice.

In other words, the "terms" and "principles" of peace, which, in the American note of November 5th, the Allies declared their readiness to accept, not only do not limit the right to claim full reparation, but affirm that right in the most ample and unqualified terms.

The American memorandum rightly admits that, "The reparation specified for in the Fourteen Points is not designed to be comprehensive."

It adds that such reparation is not in derogation of reparation due in accordance with accepted principles of international law. "Rather the Fourteen Points proceed from the basis of existing international law, and specify the further and special acts of justice necessary for a proper settlement of the war."

It is undoubtedly true that the Fourteen Points are not exhaustive, or exclusive of other reparation than that specified in them. The reparation specified in them is, as stated, limited to certain special acts of justice to Belgium, France, Serbia, and Montenegro.

The note of November 5th informed the German Government that, subject to certain qualifications, the Allied Governments "declare their willingness to make peace with the Government of Germany on the terms of peace laid down in the President's address to Congress of January 8, 1918, *and the principles of settlement enunciated in his subsequent addresses.* We must look for our principles, therefore, in the subsequent addresses as well as in the Fourteen Points.

It is necessary briefly to refer to the correspondence which preceded this note.

German and American Notes.

In a note of October 4th, the German Government asked President Wilson to take in hand the restoration of peace, and invite the belligerents to send plenipotentiaries for the purpose of opening negotiations. The German Government "accepts the programme put forth by the President of the United States in his message to Congress of January 8, 1918, *and in his latest pronouncements*—especially his speech of September 27th—*as a basis for peace negotiations."* Meanwhile an immediate armistice was asked for.

President Wilson replied in a note of October 8th. He asked for an explanation: "Does the Imperial Chancellor mean that the Imperial German Government *accepts the terms laid down* by the President in his address to the Congress of the United States on January 8th last, *and in subsequent addresses,* and that its object in entering into discussions would be only to agree upon the practical details of their application?"

Herr Solf [Foreign Secretary] replied in a note of October 19th: "The German Government has accepted the terms laid down by President Wilson in his address of January 8th, and in his subsequent addresses *as the foundation for a permanent peace of justice.* Consequently, the object of the proposed discussion would be only to come to an understanding upon practical details of the application of those terms."

After some further correspondence, President Wilson, in his note of October 23d, refers to the unreserved acceptance by the German Government of *"The terms of peace,"* laid down in his address to the Congress of the United States on January 8, 1918, and the *principles of settlement* enunciated in his subsequent addresses, particularly the address of September 27th. He cannot now refuse to take up with the Allied Governments the question of an armistice. He has, therefore, transmitted the correspondence to the Allies with the suggestion that, "*If those Governments are disposed to effect peace upon the terms and principles indicated* their military advisers should be asked to suggest terms of armistice."

The correspondence concludes with President Wilson's note of November 5th, already referred to, and was followed on November 11th by the armistice.

Fourteen Points and Subsequent Addresses.

President Wilson's address to Congress on January 8, 1918, was that in which he set out what are known as the "Fourteen Points."

The following is believed to be a complete list of the "subsequent addresses" referred to:

1. An address to Congress on February 11, 1918, in which President Wilson stated four principles to be applied in the peace settlement.

2. A Fourth-of-July address (1918) delivered at Mount Vernon, in which President Wilson stated four "ends" for which the Associated peoples of the world were fighting. And

3. An address delivered in New York on February 27, 1918, in connection with the inauguration of the Liberty Loan in which President Wilson declared certain essential principles and formulated five "particulars."

It must be observed, that throughout the correspondence with Germany, the address of January 8th and the subsequent addresses were bracketed together. The subsequent addresses are not subordinate pronouncements; they are independent speeches, addressed to different audiences, and of equal authority with the speech of January 8th. The fact that the Fourteen Points are sometimes loosely spoken of as the whole of President Wilson's peace terms must not mislead us into forgetting that the subject matter of all the negotiations was the Fourteen Points of January 8th, *and* the four points of the second address to Congress, *and* the four points of the Mount Vernon address of July 4th, *and* the declaration and the five points of the New York address of September 27th. All these have equal weight and equal authority; and all were explicitly referred to in the note of November 5th to Germany.

President Wilson's Principles.

Let us look first at the general principles laid down by the President in those pronouncements.

The first principle stated in the address to Congress of February 11th is *essential justice:*

> That each part of the final settlement must be based upon the essential justice of that particular case, and upon such adjustments as are most likely to bring a peace that will be permanent.

In the Mount Vernon address of July 4th, the following is formulated as one of the "ends for which the Associated peoples of the world are fighting and which must be conceded them before there is peace."

Honor and Respect for Law.

The consent of all nations to be governed in their conduct toward each other by the same principles of honor and of respect for the common law of civilized society that govern the individual citizens of all modern states in their relations with one another; to the end that all promises and covenants may be sacredly observed, no private plots or conspiracies hatched, no selfish injuries wrought with impunity, and a mutual trust established upon a mutual respect for right.

The Reign of Law.

President Wilson added: "These great objects can be put into a single sentence: *What we seek is the reign of law,* based upon the consent of the governed, and sustained by the organized opinion of mankind."

Lastly in the New York address of September 27th, President Wilson emphasized and elaborated this principle. He first declared that there could be no peace obtained by any kind of compromise with the Central Empires, because they were without honor and did not intend justice.

No Compromise of Principles.

He further declared:

It is of capital importance that we should also be explicitly agreed that no peace shall be obtained by any kind of compromise or abatement of the principles we have avowed as the principles for which we are fighting. There should exist no doubt about that. I am therefore going to take the liberty of speaking with the utmost frankness about the practical implications that are involved in it.

The Price to be Paid.

If it be, in deed and in truth, the common object of the Governments associated against Germany and of the nations whom they govern, as I believe it to be, to achieve by the coming settlements a secure and lasting peace, it will be necessary that all who sit down at the peace table shall come ready and willing to pay the price, the only price, that will procure it; and ready and willing also to create in some virile fashion the only instrumentality by which it can be made certain that the agreements of the peace will be honored and fulfilled. That price is impartial justice in every item of the settlement, no matter whose interest is crossed; and not only impartial justice, but also the satisfaction of the several peoples whose fortunes are dealt with. * * * But these general terms do not disclose the whole matter. Some details are needed to make them sound less like a thesis and more like a practical programme. These then are some of the particulars and I state them authoritatively as representing this Government's interpretation of its own duty with regard to peace.

The first of these particulars is that—"the impartial justice meted out must involve no discrimination between those to whom we wish to be just and those to whom we do not wish to be just. It must be a justice which plays no favorites and knows no standard but the equal rights of the several peoples concerned."

Acceptance of these Principles.

The principles thus enunciated by President Wilson are identical with the principles of justice which my colleagues and I have laid before this commission.

Take the first clause of the second address to Congress: "Each part of the final settlement must be based upon the essential justice of that particular case and upon such adjustments as are most likely to *bring peace that is permanent.*"

Take the third point of the Mount Vernon speech: The same principles of honor and respect for law between states as between individuals—"to the end that all promises and covenants may be sacredly observed, no private plots or conspiracies hatched, no selfish injuries wrought with impunity." The summing up—*"what we seek is the reign of law."*

Significance of Reign of Law.

Most significant is the phrase into which President Wilson declares that all his principles can be crystallized: "What we seek is the reign of law." The application of these words is not partial. There are no exceptions, no limitations, no qualifications. They extend to the remedying of past as well as future wrongs. President Wilson is speaking of a just peace settlement, and he does not say: "we shall seek justice in the reign of law tomorrow; let us wipe the slate as to yesterday." On the contrary, he makes it plain, both as to particulars and as to general principles, that all wrongs are to be righted, all outstanding accounts settled on the basis of justice.

Essential justice, and a permanent peace. No selfish injury wrought with impunity. What words could more aptly express the right of reparation against the aggressor for the cost of the war to the full limit of his capacity to pay?

The reign of law—and the same respect for law between nations as between individuals. To realize the significance of these words, let us turn to the civil codes of all nations—Germany included. What do they say? No wrong without a remedy. Whatever the nature of the wrong—whether to life, limb, health, property, liberty, or any other right, the wrong-doer must, as far as he can, make reparation for the wrong. As it is between individuals, so it must be between states. That is the reign of law; that is the principle of justice.

To saddle the defenders of the world's liberties with the burden is not just; it is a monstrous injustice. To compensate only some of the sufferers and leave others to bear the burden of their losses is not just. To let the wrong-doer escape payment for the damage he has wrought does not tend to a permanent peace; it encourages him to break the peace again at the first opportunity, in the sure and certain hope that even if he fails again he will not have to pay the bill.

The same great principle is emphasized even more strongly in the New York address. There can be no bargaining or compromise of principles; to achieve a secure and lasting peace, "it will be necessary that all who sit down at the peace table shall come ready and willing to pay the price, the only price, that will secure it. * * * That price is impartial justice in every item of the settlement." Impartial justice "must involve no discrimination between those to whom we wish to be just and those to whom we do not wish to be just. It must be a justice which plays no favorites and knows no standard but the equal rights of the several peoples concerned."

We have agreed to those principles. We invoke those principles. They cover full reparation for the costs of the war.

3. The American Argument.

Lastly I come to the observations which I foreshadowed on Mr. Dulles' arguments in his address today.

Reparation not Based on Contract.

Mr. Dulles speaks of the right to reparation from a defeated belligerent as resting upon "contract," because the terms imposed are set out in the treaty of peace. But to speak of contract in such a case is a misuse of terms. Contract means agreement, and implies equality of status between the parties, and a free consent. There is no question of agreement in the terms of reparation which a victorious belligerent imposes upon the enemy.

Amount Irrelevant to Principle.

Again, Mr. Dulles is concerned at the huge amount of the total war costs, and suggests that to insist on the full claim for all the Allies will prejudice the satisfaction of those states which have suffered material damage. But these considerations have nothing to do with this discussion which relates to the principles on which the reparation due by Germany is to be assessed. Presentment of the full bill for all war costs by the United States and other powers need not necessarily mean any deferment of the more urgent claims for reparation. Certain claims could always be preferred.

Distinction Between Penal Indemnity and Reparation.

Mr. Dulles also referred to a speech by Mr. Lloyd George, on January 5, 1918, in which he disclaimed the intention of demanding from Germany such an indemnity as Germany wrung from France in 1871.

Now, in the first place, that speech was made at a very dark hour for the Allies, when they might well have been prepared, for the sake of peace, to take something less than their due. But Germany did not accept those terms; she went on fighting. And in any case, what did Mr. Lloyd George say? That we would not claim such an indemnity as Germany imposed upon France—namely, an indemnity of twice the cost of the war—an indemnity of which one-half was not reparation, but penalty. We claim no penalty, but reparation only. We ask for justice, not revenge.

The following is a summary of the position:

(1) The Fourteen Points are not exhaustive as to reparation.

(2) It is admitted by the American memorandum that Belgium's full war costs must be paid, as Germany's attack on Belgium, whose neutrality she had guaranteed, was a violation of international law.

(3) Whatever rights Belgium has under international law, by reason of her neutralization, are clearly shared by those Powers who guaranteed her neutrality, and incurred fearful losses in enforcing it.

(4) The other Associated Powers (*e. g.*, United States and Italy), who helped to defend Belgian neutrality, can also claim their war costs.

(5) Therefore, even on the narrow basis of the American memorandum, reparation can be claimed for the whole war cost of the Associated Powers.

(6) But independently altogether of any question of violations of international law, full reparation is demanded by the principle of justice.

(7) The principle of justice, and the reign of law between states as between individuals, have been affirmed by President Wilson and incorporated in the terms and principles of peace accepted by the Associated Powers and by Germany, which clearly cover the demand of full reparation.

(8) Therefore, whether we apply the principles of the American memorandum, or whether we independently apply the principles formulated by President Wilson and accepted, of "the reign of law" and a just peace in either case we reach the same conclusion, that we are entitled to reparation for the full costs of the war.

Translation of Address of Mr. Klotz, French Minister of Finance, February 15, 1919.

I do not care at the moment to express a detailed opinion upon the English thesis or that of the American. The French delegation at an appropriate time will express its reasoned judgment. At the moment the debate is on a higher level.

The American delegation declines to take up the discussion on the basis accepted by the memoranda of all the other delegations. They refuse to discuss whether the principles which we have formulated, that Germany shall repair in its entirety all the damage which she has caused, is or is not in conformity with justice and with right.

Perhaps, if I may be permitted to interpret certain words, certain silences of Mr. Dulles, the American delegation would be disposed to admit the justice of our argument concerning reimbursement of the cost of the war. But in their view it is too late for such claims. The case has been tried and decided. We are in the presence of a formal contract which becomes binding on the parties and from which they are not permitted to depart.

The American argument rests upon this assertion, that there exists a contract between the Allied and Associated Powers on the one hand, and Germany on the other hand, and that the terms of this contract are such as to deny to the Allied Powers the right to claim reimbursement for their war costs. If the American delegation cannot definitely support this assertion, its argument falls, and we find ourselves guided no longer by contractual law but by justice alone.

Where, then, is the contract? In what document does it find expression?

Every contract implies reciprocal obligations and engagements. Where do we find these elements in the Allied contract? Have we, the Associated Powers, taken—impliedly let it not be forgotten—the undertaking not to demand from Germany reimbursement for the cost of the war? And what did Germany grant us in exchange? The engagement not to continue the war, to lay down their arms? It is thus in his argument that Mr. Dulles has defined the Allied contract.

We however assert, and assert in the most formal manner, that between the exchange of notes to which the American delegation refers, and where the American delegation would find the elements of a contract, and the surrender of Germany there is no relation of cause and effect. Germany surrendered on November 11th because she was conquered, and not because she found acceptable and equitable the conditions of President Wilson and of the Associated Powers. Germany, who today is trying again to raise her head, was no longer materially and morally able to reject the conditions of peace, whatever they might have been. She has indeed admitted this but recently. If the American delegation had any doubts in this respect I am certain that the opinion of General Pershing would suffice to dispel them.

Between the German Government and the Associated Powers there exists but one document which has the form and the spirit of an agreement—to employ the English phrase—and which could reasonably be called such, that is the Armistice Convention of November 11, 1918.

If the acceptance of the Fourteen Points of President Wilson, as modified by the note of November 5, 1918, as defining the future Treaty of Peace, had in the eyes of the Germans been the determining cause, the essential condition of the signature of the armistice, they would not have failed expressly so to state. If Germany had been in a position to make demands, if among other things she had been able to condition the signature of the armistice upon a declaration of the Allied Powers binding them in advance concerning the future terms of peace, Germany would not have failed to have done so. She has not done so, and this silence is alone a rebuttal of the argument presented by the American delegation.

If, then, on that date Germany had not consented at least to the minimum program of the Fourteen Points, if she had not agreed to deliver us as guarantees of safety considerable areas of territory and substantial quantities of material, the Associated Powers would without doubt have continued the war. But in the one, as in the other case, it was a question of minimum guarantees warranting the cessation of hostilities that Germany sought, that had become for her an imperative necessity.

As we were led in the course of the negotiations to formulate new demands, concerning, for instance, the occupation of the right bank of the Rhine—the armistice having been concluded for a short period only, which necessarily implies the possibility of modifying its terms, as was brilliantly argued the other day by Baron Sonnino—so, too, we have not for an instant considered that from several points of view we were no longer bound by the armistice contract of November 11th. As in the case of the Rhineland, we are justified in formulating demands which are not perhaps expressly included in the Fourteen Points of President Wilson, but which are based, as we are ready to show, on justice and on right. And we will not have to support these claims on the basis of public international law as appealed to by the American delegation, which law unfortunately is derived but too often from precedents of force and violence, but on the "common law" of civilized nations, to which in three points of his address of July 4th, which address is also included by reference in the note of November 5th, President Wilson referred in the following terms:

The things for which the Associated peoples of the world are fighting, and which must be conceded them before there is peace, are the following: * * *

The consent of all nations to be governed in their conduct toward each other by the same principles of honcr and of respect for the common law of civilized society that govern the individual citizens of all modern states in their relations with one another; to the end that all promises and covenants may be sacredly observed, no private plots or conspiracies hatched, no selfish injuries wrought with impunity, and a mutual trust established upon a mutual respect for right.

Today what would the American delegation have us admit—that we have impliedly renounced recourse to this common law; that by our silence we have agreed that our nation, ravaged in 1871, assaulted, invaded, systematically sacked today, should accept, and that the nation responsible for all of these wrongs should be freed from, the most terrible financial burden that any European nation has ever known? And that our statesmen and generals meeting at Versailles have conceded without discussion and without debate that victorious France should be a ruined France, crushed for a century, perhaps forever? I cannot accept that unless it is proved.

I am in a position to give evidence on another point, having taken part in the work at Versailles on the 2d and 4th of last November.

If, in my opinion, there is no contract in accordance with which I have waived my rights to reimbursement for certain categories of expenses resulting from the war, on the other hand there does exist a contract by the terms of which I have expressly reserved these rights.

I have said that between the Allies and Germany there is but one written document which has up till now been signed, having the form and giving rise to the legal relations of a contract. This is the armistice convention of November 11, 1918, between the Allied and Associated Powers represented by Marshal Foch and Admiral Wemyss and the German delegation.

Now, as to the question which we are discussing, does this document contain any express reservation of our rights? Is it there specified that as concerns reparation of damage we have in advance tied our hands?

Let us open this agreement to the chapter entitled "Financial Clauses," the terms of which were by us carefully considered, weighed, and formulated. They were not hastily written. What are the first words? How is the first phrase drafted?

XIX. Reserving all subsequent claims and demands on the part of the Allies and of the United States, reparation of damage.

Here is something clear.

Our rights are reserved as to all "subsequent claims and demands."

We have before us an express clause, which implies no limitation of our rights, which stipulates a full reservation of all our rights, particularly as concerns "reparation of damage."

Let it not be argued that this is a phrase which has regard exclusively to the armistice and the obligation of which was to be limited to the armistice. At that time an armistice of a month only was anticipated. It could not then have been thought that complete reparation of the damage caused by the war could have been brought about even during successive renewals of the armistice. The reservation clearly contemplated the future treaty and the negotiations which would result in its signature.

Nor can it be said that this reservation contemplates exclusively such claims and demands as are contained in the Fourteen Points of President Wilson modified in accordance with the declaration of the Allies of November 5th. If this declaration of November 5th had in fact constituted a contract binding the Associated Powers and Germany, what occasion, what necessity would there have been to refer to it in the Armistice Convention?

That which exists, that to which I hold, that to which I have a right to hold, is the fact that in a contract between the Allied Powers and Germany we have reserved our rights in reference to the finan cial clauses and the reparation of damage "as to all future claims and demands."

Therefore I have the honor to call on you to proclaim our right to integral reparation. You will see later how by agreement this right shall be applied. We will consider whether it is wise to exert our right to the full. We will settle the question of the priority of certain claims, a priority recognized I trust by all of the states represented here. We will then have settled the principles which will permit our sub-commissions to undertake a useful work.

Address on Behalf of the American Delegates. By John Foster Dulles, Esq., on February 19, 1919.

Mr. President:

The very illuminating and instructive debate of recent days has brought forward certain arguments, which, unless they can be disposed of, seriously affect the validity of the principles proposed by the American delegation. Mr. Loucheur frankly expresses the view that the structure of our case had been demolished, and, with remarkable penetration of thought and clarity of expression, he has analyzed our discussions to date and had laid before you three considerations which in his mind, disturb considerably the American principles. These are:

The argument of the Hon. Mr. Hughes, based on the violation of the neutrality of Belgium.

The argument of the Hon. Mr. Klotz, based on Article XIX of the armistice of November 11.

The argument of the Hon. Mr. Protchitch, relative to the difference in the situation as regards Germany on the one hand and Austria-Hungary, Bulgaria, and Turkey on the other hand.

It was the opinion of Mr. Loucheur, and I confess it is my own, that these constitute the three serious arguments which have been directed against the American case as originally presented. I would have desired in any event to reply to these arguments, and I welcome the clear analysis made by Mr. Loucheur which, sweeping away irrelevant matter, has crystallized the situation and presented it in concise and lucid form.

Let me first, in a word or two, restate the American proposition, in order that the full force and relevancy of the objections thereto may be clear in our minds.

The American statement of principles is based on the fundamental proposition that we are not here to create new rights; that we are here, to use the words which have received authoritative sanction, "to consider the details of the application" of existing rights. To determine what these rights are, we turn first to what we regard as an agreement between the Associated Governments and Germany as to the terms of peace. We give what we believe to be a fair construction of this agreement. We also note that this agreement does not waive rights which may have come into being previously in accordance with accepted principles of international law. We accordingly regard these rights as existing and to be enforced. The practical result of our conclusion is that *by agreement* Germany is liable to make compensation for all damage done to the civilian population of the Allies and their property by the aggression of Germany by land, by sea, and from the air; that *by operation of law* those who have been the victim of admittedly illegal acts, such as the violation of Belgium, the torpedoing of merchant vessels without warning, the inhumane treatment of prisoners of war, etc., etc., are entitled to reparation.

Having thus attempted hastily to reconstruct the American case before your eyes, let us now consider the effect thereon of the argument which Mr. Loucheur has so ably epitomized.

Let me first deal with the argument of the honorable delegate for Serbia. He says that not having reached any agreement with Austria-Hungary, Bulgaria, or Turkey, as to what the terms of peace with these countries shall be, we are free to endeavor to impose any such terms as we decide to be just. In a technical sense this may be correct. I am unable to point to any signed document whereby the nations at war with Austria-Hungary, Bulgaria, and Turkey agreed with these nations as to what the reparation terms of peace should be. I do maintain, however, that it was understood that the settlement with these countries was to be in the spirit of the terms specifically agreed to as to Germany and which were originally enunciated as the terms of a general peace. I doubt that Serbia herself is prepared to renounce the right to appeal to those terms as embodying the principles which should govern the settlement of her war with Austria-Hungary. But if we accept the argument of the honorable delegate of Serbia, what is its implication? It is said that the agreement as to the terms of peace relates only to Germany; therefore, as to others we are free. By the same token, however, as to Germany we are not free. We are not free because we have specifically agreed among ourselves and with Germany what the terms of peace shall be.

This assertion leads me to a discussion of the point which Mr. Klotz developed and which, if I understand right, was to the effect that we have no agreement with Germany as to the terms of peace. To quote his words: "There exists only one document which has the form and the spirit of a contract, of an agreement, and which can legitimately be described as such. That document is the Armistice Covenant of November 11, 1918."

Gentlemen, this is a serious assertion, the consequences of which, if it be accepted, are momentous It means that where we thought we had a chart, we have none.

I have taken the liberty of circulating among you a fairly complete abstract of the correspondence with Germany leading up to the armistice of November 11, 1918. If you will refresh your recollection as to this correspondence, you will see that Germany initiated the discussion by a request for an armistice, which request the German Government asked the President of the United States to transmit to his associates. The President of the United States refused to transmit such a request until all of the interested parties should be in complete agreement as to the basic terms of peace. The President even went so far as to refuse to consider an armistice on the understanding that a certain program should be "the basis for peace discussion." The President insisted on the withdrawal of this phrase and the substitution in lieu thereof of the phrase "terms of peace," as to which discussion would be limited to "the practical details of their application." The President transmitted this correspondence to the Allies, who replied that they were willing to make peace on the terms specified, with two qualifications, one of which was a clarification of the term specifying the compensation which should be made by Germany. This understanding was accepted by the President and communicated to Germany. Then—and then only—was the German Government advised that an armistice would be considered. You will thus see, gentlemen, that there were two series of negotiations—one as to the terms of peace, the other as to the terms of armistice—and that until there was agreement as to the terms of peace, consideration of an armistice was postponed. I cannot believe that Mr. Klotz now seriously contends that no agreement came into being when the Allies, after carefully considering this correspondence which had passed between the United States and Germany, stated: "They declare their willingness to make peace with the German Government on the terms of peace laid down by the President's address to Congress of January, 1918, and the principles of settlement enunciated in his subsequent address." I assert that there is in that declaration the spirit—nay, more, the form and substance of an agreement. We find every element legally necessary to constitute a binding contract. We have a proposal by one party, a negotiation leading to a change of terms, and a final acceptance by all, in reliance on which all of the parties, not only Germany, but the United States and others, have changed their position.

But I do not, I am sure, have to resort to a textbook of law and prove the existence of a legal agreement. This is not a transaction between petty merchants. When great France, in that critical hour and with issues of world-wide importance at stake, solemnly and in conjunction with her Allies, said to the United States for its guidance and for transmission to Germany: "We will make peace on specific terms," I know that the United States, that the world, can count upon France making peace on these terms.

So I cannot believe that I have understood Mr. Klotz aright in this matter and that France regards itself as free to propose terms other than those adopted by her on November 4, 1918. I feel that it must rather be the thought of Mr. Klotz that the armistice agreement, occurring after the agreement as to the terms of peace, in some way modified this binding engagement which she had assumed.

Let us consider this possibility. In the first place, as I have pointed out, the negotiations relative to the terms of peace, and the negotiations relative to an armistice, constituted two distinct series of negotiations. The Associated Powers were one in a determination not to consider an armistice until there should be complete agreement as to the terms of peace. Accordingly, although it was on October 6, 1918, that the German Government asked for an armistice, it was only on November 5th, after complete agreement had been reached as to the terms of peace, that the German Government was notified that armistice commissioners would be received. Is it, therefore, conceivable that the armistice could control and govern the terms of peace? Is it conceivable that the Associated Governments would have prolonged the war for a month to secure an agreement as to terms of peace, which agreement six days later was to be nullified by an armistice formulated by military advisers?

It appears clearly throughout the correspondence, copies of which are before you, that it was understood that the armistice was peculiarly a matter for military advisers. The terms of peace were first settled by the highest political authorities of the Associated Governments. Had Marshal Foch and Admiral Wemyss, great as were their positions, power to amend and overrule by the armistice which they signed terms of peace which had previously been agreed to by President Wilson, Mr. Orlando, Mr. Lloyd George and Mr. Clemenceau? Obviously not. The armistice was, as the diplomatic correspondence shows it was to be, a military instrument framed by military advisers. But did Marshal Foch and Admiral Wemyss misconstrue their authority; did they purport to introduce into the armistice provisions which would modify the terms of peace to which their superiors had previously agreed? Such action, if they took it, could not be binding. But it is clear that they did not take it.

The armistice says that, reserving all rights as to future claims and demands, certain gold and securities are to be delivered up. Why was this reservation made? Obviously not to modify or affect the terms of peace, but to insure that, as a military and interim measure, further deliveries could be demanded. The right so reserved has been exercised subsequently in renewals of the armistice which require additional surrenders of property by Germany. If, therefore, we are here sitting as an armistice commission, I fully agree that we could consider the desirability of requiring further deliveries of goods by Germany, and exercise the rights reserved in the armistice of November 11th; but we are not the armistice commission. We are the peace commission. It is not our duty to construe and to apply the terms of the military armistice, but the peace terms. Accordingly, for the purpose of our discussion here, the armistice is irrelevant. Our duty here is to determine the practical details of the application of the agreed terms of peace. We accordingly turn back to those terms of peace, and I appeal to Mr. Klotz to reaffirm the solemn declaration of his Government, made on November 4, 1918, that France is willing to make peace with Germany on the terms then specified. If he does reaffirm that declaration, he must then be prepared to consider with me, not the terms of armistice, but the "terms of peace."

So much, gentlemen, for the argument based on the terms of armistice. There is left now for consideration the third proposition, that enunciated by the Hon. Mr. Hughes, to the effect that independently of any agreement as to the terms of peace, the Associated Governments are entitled to recover war costs through the operation of the principle that rights which arose by operation of law, upon the doing of an illegal act, are not waived and can be enforced.

The discussion so far has been on a judicial basis, and I am sure I shall not be subject to criticism if I keep it on that basis. Accordingly, I propose to consider for a moment where Mr. Hughes' argument logically leads us. To this end I apply the universally accepted principle that to warrant reparation of damage for an illegal act, there must be a causol relationship between the illegal act and the alleged damage. In the case of what countries can there be claimed to be a causal relationship between the violation of Belgium and general war costs? Great Britain based its declaration of war on the violation of Belgian neutrality, and I accordingly concede that it is arguable that the war costs of the British Empire are attributable to this act. But this cannot be said of the war costs of France. War came to France as a result of the declaration of war against her by Germany. The invasion of Belgium was but an incident to the prosecution of this war against France which had previously been determined upon. The war costs of Italy cannot be alleged to bear any relationship to the invasion of Belgium. The same is true of Serbia, of Greece, of Rumania, of Czechoslovakia, of Poland, of Russia, of Japan, of the United States. Only in the case of Belgium and of Great Britain is it even arguable that there is a causal relationship between war costs as a whole and the invasion of Belgium. Having thus clarified the scope and application of the doctrine enunciated by Mr. Hughes, let us consider its validity even in this limited sphere.

Now, gentlemen, the question of the proper construction and the legal effect of the Treaty of London of 1839 is one which we could discuss for many months and then possibly not find ourselves in agreement. I do not wish to involve the commission in these difficult questions of construction. I will merely suggest to you one of several reasons why, in my opinion, the argument of Mr. Hughes is not sound. The Treaty of 1839 is in form a treaty for the benefit of Belgium. Mr. Hughes treats it as such. Historically, it had its birth in that understanding. Belgium desired to secure certain frontiers which would be strategically sound. The then five great Powers were unwilling to grant her those frontiers, but in exchange for the acceptance by Belgium of restricted frontiers, agreed to insure Belgian neutrality. The treaty thus constitutes what, in the common law, is known as a beneficiary contract, or contract for the benefit of a third party. This means then that when Great Britain, France, Russia, Austria, and Prussia agreed to disenable themselves from making war on Belgium, the benefit of that agreement ran in favor of Belgium alone. Accordingly, when Germany made war upon Belgium that was an illegal act—illegal, that is, in respect to Belgium, who was the beneficiary of the contract that war would not be made. Any special position, therefore, that results from a violation by Germany of its covenant made to the benefit of Belgium redounds to the benefit of Belgium, and not to the benefit of the other contracting powers.

That Great Britain may have been under a duty, moral or legal, to come to the aid of Belgium does not modify in any degree our conclusion that the benefits of the treaty ran in favor of Belgium. If Great Britain, in 1839, assumed an obligation, she did so in pursuance of what she then regarded as adequate consideration, and the performance of that duty could not give rise to a special right. Mr. Hughes stated, "Great Britain and France may be compared to the policeman whose sworn task is to prevent a breach of the law." Precisely—but does the policeman receive his hire from the wrongdoer when he arrests? No; in making the arrest the policeman has but performed his duty—nobly, gallantly, at great sacrifice, if you will, but still his duty. And the reparation made by the wrongdoer is made to the victim—not to the guardian of the law.

Gentlemen, I will not weary you with a further discussion of the legal technicalities of beneficiary contracts. Nor will I develop the rule as to indirect damage which, if applied as it has uniformly been applied in international decisions, notably in the Alabama case, would nullify Mr. Hughes' conclusion, even if I am wrong as to the construction of the treaty of 1839. I pass to apply the test of the relative reasonableness of our conclusions. If the argument which I make is sound, it leads to the conclusion that Belgium stands in a special position by reason of Germany's breach of her covenant not to make war on Belgium. That is a conclusion which has been accepted by the whole world, even including Germany, which formally admitted the illegality of its action in respect of Belgium and the duty of making full reparation therefor. If the argument of Mr. Hughes is sound, it leads to the conclusion that Great Britain, and Great Britain alone, shares the special position of Belgium. This is a conclusion so extraordinary that the Hon. Mr. Hughes, with that common sense and bigness of heart for which he is noted, was compelled to repudiate it. What form did his repudiation take? Did he say: My conclusion is unsound, therefore I must have reached it by unsound processes of thought? No; he said: My conclusion is absurd; therefore, I will multiply it by ten and the absurdity will disappear. After adopting reasoning which if sound led to the establishment of a special privilege for Great Britain in respect of war costs, he illogically but with a generosity which we can but admire invited us all to come and share it.

Gentlemen, if we hold to the domain of reason, we cannot adopt such methods. It is clear that under no principle of international law has Germany become our debtor for the general costs of the war. Any such right, if it is to exist, can be created only by agreement. So we are forced back again, inevitably, irresistibly, to the proceedings of November 4th, and the statement of the Associated Governments that they were willing to make peace with Germany on certain terms. There is our agreement. It provides, and the Allies took special steps to specify it: "Compensation will be made by Germany for all damage done to all civilian population of the Allies and their property by the aggression of Germany by land, by sea, and from the air." That is our agreement. It is not a basis of discussion—it is a term of peace. It does not provide for the expense to Governments of maintaining military establishments.

There, gentlemen, are my answers to what Mr. Loucheur stated to be the only serious attack on the American position. I have given these answers sincerely, frankly, as I see the right.

It is not agreeable for me to stand here as proponent of an argument which seems, even in principle, to be in the interest of Germany. I say "even in principle" because I believe that the propositions enunciated by the American delegation are, practically, those which will secure the maximum of reparation and its most equitable distribution. To demand the gigantic total of war costs would, I agree with Mr. Van Den Heuvel, be to jeopardize securing that specific reparation as to which Germany must clearly recognize her liability, and the satisfaction of which will tax her resources to the limit. But even so, the American delegation would not be participating actively in this debate did we not feel that vital principles were involved. In a material sense we stand to gain, gain greatly, by the defeat of our proposition. But we did not make war for material interests. We do not make peace for material interests. We have sacrificed, and today again stand ready to sacrifice, our material interests for principles which we have espoused. I stand here today—honestly convinced that we are bound by an agreement and that no other course is honorably open to us than that which I have proposed.

In saying this, I do not mean to suggest for a moment that there is any delegation here actuated by different motives. I recognize the existence of an honest disagreement. The American delegation has listened open-mindedly to the discussion ready to be convinced of the errors of their ways. We have not been convinced. Accordingly I have tried to convince you. I hope I have succeeded. If not, may I submit this suggestion: Our debate has revolved around the meaning of the declaration of November 4, 1918. The gentlemen who drafted that declaration, who discussed it, who adopted it, are here with us. I propose, gentlemen, that we ask them their understanding as to the meaning and legal effect of that document.

Whatever we do here is, in any event, subject to review and I seriously question whether a decision on such important questions of principle as have been discussed here is within the competence of this commission. If you will refer to the resolution creating this commission, you will find nothing empowering us to determine basic principles. This commission was created "to examine and report on the question of the amount for reparation which the enemy countries should pay, and are capable of paying, as well as the form in which payment should be made." And I think it was added, "to recommend measures to guarantee payment." It was thus evidently assumed by the commission, as, in fact, they had reason to assume, that the terms of peace were settled and that all we had to do was to "determine the practical details of their application." It appears that this is not the case, but that there are important, indeed, fundamental differences of opinion relative to principle. I therefore propose that we should cease discussion here and refer back to the Supreme War Council the question of whether, in their opinion, war costs are properly to be included in the bill for reparation to be presented to the enemy. Pending their reply we can proceed with the other pressing work which is before us, and which the world demands should be expeditiously dealt with.

Treatment of Private Property.

The question of the treatment of private rights is dealt with in the German delegation's notes of the 22d and 29th of May and in the Annex No. 1 to their Remarks on the Conditions of Peace. In addition, the general objections set out in these documents are reproduced under different forms in various parts of the Remarks.

QUESTIONS OF PRINCIPLE.

The objections of principle to the Conditions of Peace put forward by the German delegation on this subject may be summed up as follows:

(a) It is not legitimate to use the private property of German nationals to meet the obligations of Germany.

(b) The settlement of private rights is not made on the principle of reciprocity.

(c) German property should not be used as a guarantee for the liabilities of the states allied to Germany.

(d) The liquidations to be made by the Allied and Associated Powers, in depriving the owner of the free disposition of his property, are of a confiscatory character.

The answers of the Allied and Associated Powers to these objections are as follows:

(a) As regards the first objection, they would call attention to the clear acknowledgment by Germany of a pecuniary obligation to the Allied and Associated Powers, and to the further circumstance that the immediate resources of Germany are not adequate to meet that obligation. It is the clear duty of Germany to meet the admitted obligation as fully and as promptly as possible and to that end to make use of all available means. The foreign investments of German nationals constitute a class of assets which are readily available. To these investments the treaty simply requires Germany to make prompt resort.

It is true that, as a general principle, a country should endeavour to avoid making use of the property of a part of its nationals to meet state obligations; but conditions may arise when such a course becomes necessary. In the present war Allied Powers themselves have found it necessary to take over foreign investments of their nationals to meet foreign obligations, and have given their own domestic obligations to the nationals who have been thus called upon to take a share, by this use of their private property, in meeting the obligations of the state.

The time has arrived when Germany must do what she has forced her opponents to do. The necessity for the adoption of this course by Germany is clearly understood by the German peace delegates, and is accepted by them in the following passage, quoted textually from their note of the 22d of May:

> The German peace delegation is conscious of the fact that under the pressure of the burden arising from the peace treaty on the whole future of German economic life, German property in foreign countries cannot be maintained to its previous extent. On the contrary, Germany, in order to meet her pecuniary obligations, will have to sacrifice this property abroad in wide measure. She is prepared to do so.

The fundamental objection mentioned above is completely answered by the note itself.

(b) The German delegation maintains in its note of the 22d of May that there is only the appearance of reciprocity in regard to the settlement of enemy property, and this objection is developed in the Annex to the Remarks. The objection, however, arises from a confusion between two entirely different matters. As regards exceptional war measures taken in the different countries in respect of enemy property, there is a reciprocal provision, these exceptional war measures being confirmed on both sides. Quite a different matter is that of the mode in which enemy property shall be dealt with thereafter. German property, as is admitted in the German note, must serve towards meeting Germany's obligations to the Allies. The compensation to the

German property owner must be made by Germany itself. In this respect there can be no question of reciprocity.

(c) On the question whether German property should serve as a guarantee for the liabilities of the states allied with Germany, it is to be observed, on the one hand, that the actions of Germany and her allies during the war have given rise to complete solidarity between these Powers from the economic standpoint. For instance, negotiations undertaken without scruple between Germany and her allies have resulted in the division between these countries of the proceeds of the Allied and Associated property liquidated contrary to all right in the territories occupied by the German troops. Further, the German authorities have in several ways treated the Allied and Associated Powers as being jointly concerned. For instance, they have seized French credit balances in Belgian banks as a measure of reprisal against acts done in other Allied states. They have similarly justified the liquidation of French property in Germany on the ground that similar measures have been taken against German property in other Allied countries. Thus, the principle of joint liability to which Germany now objects has been initiated by herself, and she has created a situation which does not permit the Allied and Associated Powers in practice to separate the obligations of her allies from her own. Nevertheless the Allied and Associated Powers are prepared to omit from the charge on the property of German nationals the liability to satisfy the unpaid debts of nationals of Powers allied with Germany.

(d) The method of using this property laid down by the treaty cannot be considered, either in principle or in the method of its application, as a measure of confiscation. Private German interests will only be injured by the measures contemplated so far as Germany may decide that they shall be, since all the proceeds of German property will be carried to the credit of Germany, who is required to compensate her own nationals, and will go to reduce her debt to the Allied and Associated Powers.

Contracts.

"Most of the other countries have insisted upon a general plan by which contracts existing before the war, between their nationals and nationals of Germany, shall be generally canceled. There are some exceptions like pecuniary liabilities; and some special kinds of contracts like insurance are otherwise treated. The United States, Brazil, and Japan, however, have not adhered to this plan, and are expressly excepted from its operation.

"In the United States many contracts were dissolved, under our laws, by the state of war. Examples are: partnerships; contracts requiring communication with the enemy; and, under decisions of our courts, contracts the performance of which was rendered unjust or inequitable on account of the changed conditions produced by the state of war. Other contracts were merely suspended. These last would be revived automatically under our laws, at the end of the war, and, so far as the United States is concerned, are treated as revived in this draft.

"The dissolution of all contracts, which are now merely suspended, would entail great confusion and hardship upon many persons and businesses, including both those of the United States and of Germany; it would not seem just to cancel such contracts without the consent of the owners.

"The other countries represented on the Economic Commission have appreciated the position of the

United States in this respect and have consented that this country, as well as Brazil and Japan, should leave unchanged the legal status of contracts to which their nationals are parties.

"Provision is made, however, in Article I, whereby nationals of all the Allied and Associated countries, the United States included, shall have access to a new tribunal with a neutral president, so that they need not be compelled to resort to German courts for the adjudication of their contractual rights after the war."

INDEX